The Complete Keto Diet Meal Prep Instant Pot Cookbook

Low-Carb, High-Fat & Time-Saving Ketogenic Diet Instant Pot Recipes For Busy People

Jaime Thomas

ISBN: 978-1721922796

This document is geared towards providing exact and reliable information in regards to the topic and issue covered. The publication is sold with the idea that the publisher is not required to render accounting, officially permitted, or otherwise, qualified services. If advice is necessary, legal or professional, a practiced individual in the profession should be ordered.

Disclaimer Notice:

Please note the information contained within this document is for educational and entertainment purposes only. Every attempt has been made to provide accurate, up to date and reliable complete information. No warranties of any kind are expressed or implied. Readers acknowledge that the author is not engaging in the rendering of legal, financial, medical or professional advice.

The content of this book has been derived from various sources. Please consult a licensed profe sional before attempting any techniques outlined in this book.

By reading this document, the reader agrees that under no circumstances are is the author responsible for any loses, direct or indirect, which are incurred as a result the use of infor- mation contained within this document, including, but not limited to, - errors, omissions, or inaccuracies.

CONTENTS

INTRODUCTION

If you have ever had the feeling that your life has become dominated by activities revolving around working and organizing food, and a typical week consists of waking up in the morning, rushing to work, commuting, working, hasty lunch break, commuting home, eating dinner, running errands. Then you may have noticed there's not much time left for anything else. And what about money flowing out of your wallet to satisfy your food whims?

Can't resist buying from a burger stand or dropping in to a bakery for a croissant? The world doesn't end if you do so once in a while, but if added up, you may quickly realize you are spending lots of money on stuff you could easily do without.

We may argue that's just the way life is or not, but one thing is for sure - it does't take much to make it way better. Planning meals in an organized way for the whole week (or more) may sound like a big investment, but in reality, it saves us a lot of time and money.

How much happier would your family, partner, or friends then be? How much would you develop yourself, having more time to follow a passion or hobby? How much more money would there be left in your pocket if you stopped spending it randomly whenever you have a whim.

If you start wondering if a conventional cookbook could offer you so much, the answer is simple - NO. Not a conventional one. But this Keto Diet Meal Prep cookbook – oh YES!

Whether we like it or not, our world is accelerating and new forms or cooking are coming out. This book is a culinary response to that acceleration and modern people's needs. Let's begin.

What to expect from this cookbook

The pages of this cookbook will be guiding you through the whole process of Meal prep, how to follow the Keto Diet and how to get the most out of both using your electric pressure cooker. You will learn how to organize yourself, get everything ready and what is the actual cooking process like.

You will learn what meal prep is and how it will transform the way that you eat. Furthermore, I will explain how to get on this journey without feeling overwhelmed or unmotivated. Next, you will learn everything you need to know about the Ketogenic Diet, it's pros and cons. I will aslo give you the reasons why your Instant Pot pressure cooker will take your meal prep to the next level, and how you can use it to create awesome, delicious and easy keto meals.

Finally, I will present you plenty of exciting and inspiring keto diet meal prep recipes that will cover all your daily meals and needs, taking you to the extraordinary lifystyle you have always dreamed of.

You will also learn plenty of tips that will help you cook your meal prep meals in the most efficient way, and also you will learn how to use your Instant Pot in the best possible way.

So grab your Instant Pot, this keto diet meal prep cookbook and some groceries and you let's start your best culinary journey ever - the meal prepping!

Let's get into it!

WHAT REALLY IS MEAL PREP?

A solution in the era of constant rush.

Meal Prep or Meal Preparation is about cooking dishes in advance for a few days or for a week in order to save time and streamline your healthy eating habits. Major idea is to cook a big portion of one kind of food and divided it into parts, pack into plastic containers and store in the fridge or freezer.

Meal Prep is very helpful for everyone: busy people find it easier to cook dinner once a week, because they simply have too tight schedule during the week-days; sportsmen cook in advance in order to control intakes of fats, proteins, carbohydrates; dieting individuals monitors their calories intake; people on a low budget prefer Meal Prep, because it is the most economical way of eating. This list can be endless because Meal Prep is a versatile tool to schedule your breakfast, lunches and dinners, as well as make your nutrition more wholesome.

When you prepare your meals in advance, you will never skip your breakfast, just because you overslept and are late for work. You will forget about eating cheap fast food during the day, because you will have your homemade healthy lunch box. And finally, Meal Prep will make your evenings better: instead of cooking your dinner after work during an hour, you will be able to enjoy tasty dish as soon as you cross the threshold of your home.

WHAT ARE THE BENEFITS FOR YOU?

From planning meals to planning life.

A great positive side effect of meal prepping is that you learn how to organize your life better.

The first step is to plan your shopping carefully. If you have never used shopping lists before, it's perhaps time to start. That will help you adjust meals and portions accordingly. You will learn how to prepare and eat just enough without having leftovers or overeating. If you prepare meals for the whole family, you will save yourself the trouble of preparing different food two or even three times a day and then cleaning it all up. The alternative beign eating out, and that's expensive and most of the time - unhealthy.

Planning your meals develops you as a person because once taken care of, that skill may go beyond cooking and will surely help you organize your life better.

The Long Desired Weight Loss is Finally Easy to Achieve

Now when you have the whole-day schedule prepared, you are less likely to snack outside the schedule. Having a general plan for anything in life strongly builds a sense of discipline.

Therefore, if you combine meal prepping with appropriate nutrition, you will create an excellent lifestyle where weight loss is not a goal itself, but merely a means to an end. You will not have to obsessively focus on counting, yet you will see results soon enough. No more calories count, weight loss, or how I refere to it as stay fit, will be easier than ever.

Losing weight happens automatically as a side effect of eating appropriate, schedule- based meals.

Eat Clean! No Room for Junk Food Anymore

Through organizing your meals, you greatly decrease the risk of snacking on unhealthy, processed food and fast foods that's literally shouting from every corner of the city.

Having prepared meals, you quickly notice that even if you fancy some grab-and-go tacos or a burger, you will not go for it. Getting food from vending machines will also become a thing of the past. And, of course, you are much less likely to throw out something you spent time and money on.

You will quickly realize that meal prep makes you a healthier person. When you eat cleaner, you feel better, more energetic, disciplines and you not only have a sense of control over your life, but also this type of food prepping, is a the key to long-term happiness. Think of the food as your fuel and of yourself as a top class luxurious car. Would you fuel it with low-quality gas that could damage the engine? Probably not. Meal prepping forces you to skip low-quality fuel and treat your engine better.

Nutritional Education

If you want to become an excellent meal planner, basic knowledge about food will come in very handy. Knowing how to compose a balanced meal is not that difficult. A proper content of proteins, fats, and carbohydrates in an adequate ratio will help you remain satiated for a longer period of time. As a result, hunger pangs will diminish and you will stop snacking on foods your body doesn't really need.

You may not only develop a genuine interest in healthy eating habits, but you will be challenged to learn how to pack and store food properly. Simple as it sounds, a bit of know-how is necessary.

Last but not least, labelling pre-made meals will keep your food organized and make sure you have control over the freshness. Meal prepping does not mean eating stale food.

TIPS FOR A GREAT START

1. *PLAN AHEAD. PICK A DAY AND STICK TO IT.*

   Sunday is considered the best day to prepare food for the whole week.
   Draw up a list of meals and days, and have it on a piece of paper. That never fails.
   You can easily print meal planners from the internet, which may be an excellent
   solution here.Better yet, learn to plan two or even three weeks ahead and you find
   the perfect balance and meal prepping days for you.

2. *GO FOR DIVERSITY*

   That means not repeating the same dish seven times a week. That would be too
   boring and unhealthy at the same time. Prepare two to three alternatives so you
   avoid nutritional burn-out. It may be something as simple as changing the source
   of proteins (i.e. meat for fish or tofu) or a different type of vegetables.

3. *MAKE A LIST BEFORE SHOPPING*

   This will train you to stick to the plan, not toss impulse items into your cart. You will
   save money and time and keep yourself from buying junk food, however crispy it
   may be. If something's not in your fridge, you will not eat it.

4. *KEEP IT SIMPLE*

   Although trying more difficult recipes is most welcome, I recommend that at the
   beginning you stick to simple recipes. Over time, as you become more adept, you
   may increase the complexity or try your own recipes.

5. *COOK MORE ITEMS AT ONCE, WHENEVER POSSIBLE.*

   A good example of that would be roasting a couple of things in the oven or on the
   stove. It's not only time saving, but your electricity bill will look way better.

6. *INVEST IN GOOD-QUALITY CONTAINERS AND MASON JARS.*

   These will help you store things longer without risk of wasting food, and they look
   fancy. Eating from such containers makes things taste better.
   I would also recommend buying larger pots and frying pans

7. *BUY PRE-CUT VEGETABLES*

   Even though they may be a bit more expensive, they make your life easier and will
   save you additional time and efforts.

8. *DRINK LOTS OF WATER*

It may sound really obvious, but very often we confuse hunger pangs with dehydration. Water fills your stomach and **you do not feel hunger, which makes it a real basis of each diet.**

WHAT TO AVOID

- Processed and/or packaged foods like pasta, certain types of cheese, pizzas

- Processed and/or packaged meat

- Vegetable oils

- Soft drinks and sugary beverages

- All kinds of crackers, cookies, cakes, and pastries

- Candy bars

- All kinds of fast foods, including French Fries and Chips

- White bread made of processed white wheat-flour

- Margarine

- Energy drinks

- Ice creams

- MSG and other toxic additives

All things are difficult before they become easy.

The concept of meal prep is to maintain a healthy lifestyle in a rushing environment. The idea offers the wisdom of not taking the easy way out and eating junk food tempting us everywhere we go. Instead, we learn to take responsibility for what we eat and what we become as a result. Given this, the Keto diet offers one of the best posibilities to eat healthy without losing time and energy cooking every day, even twice a day.

These keto recipes are meant to help you initiate the changes and go through the tough beginning. But remember, things seem dificult until you make them seem easy. The results will be well worth the time. No doubt about it.

This book is an investment that pays huge interests quickly without forcing you to spend a lot of money at the beginning. It's really simple to follow and the results are guaranteed.

Your success is entirely dependent on your determination to stick to the plan and give up on toxic things you considered normal before.

The Keto Meal Prep Instant Pot Recipes in the book are predominantly easy and perfect for beginners. Advanced cooking freaks will definitely find something for themselves as well.

Buddha said, "To enjoy good health, to bring true happiness to one's family, to bring peace to all, one must first discipline and control one's own mind." In order to take any action, we first need to realize the importance of our diet and how it affects the temples our bodies are. Love the life you have while enjoying the journey to a better and healthier nutrition.

GOING KETO

The Ketogenic diet is undoubtedly the most controversial one today. And while there are tons of successful stories that prove to us that the secret to healthy living and weight maintaining indeed lies in ditching the carbs, many people are scared to approach such a strict eating plan.

Won't all that fat raise my cholesterol levels? Won't butter and bacon widen my waist? Will I hurt my health if I enter ketosis? The answer? A definite **NO**.

DOES IT REALLY WORK?

Definitely! Ask anyone who has been motivated enough to stick to this diet's guidelines and you will get the same answer – the Keto diet will help you lose or maintain weight in the healthiest way possible without sacrificing your full tummy or your satisfied taste buds.

The main point of the Ketogenic diet is to steer clear of carbohydrates and instead, train your body to run on fat. It may seem impossible at this point, but this is very achievable.

Think of your body as a car with a backup tank. When the petrol runs out, your car will use the fuel from the gas tank to keep on moving. Your body works in a similar way. Once you empty your glucose reserves (as we know that carbohydrates get broken down into glucose), your body will turn to your reserved fat for energy.

What Is Ketosis and Is It Dangerous?

The moment that your body starts to use fat for energy, it enters the state of ketosis. During the food conversion fat gets broken down into ketones (hence the name ketogenic), and the goal of this diet is to use the ketones for energy instead of glucose.

Many confuse the state of ketosis with diabetic ketosis, which is something else entirely, and think that it is dangerous. Instead, it is just an indicator that your carb ditching has not been in vain and that you are on the right path to weight loss and lasting health.

How to Know if It's Working?

If you have reached ketosis, that means that you have been following the right Ketogenic guidelines. You will know that you are in the state of ketosis if you are experiencing fatigue, rapid weight loss, or bad breath.

These symptoms may not sound appealing but they will only bother you for about 2 weeks or so, since that is the average time that the human body needs in order to adapt to the new source of energy.

What Are the Ketogenic Guidelines?

The Ketogenic diet has gotten the bad reputation for being hard to follow thanks to its strict macro recommendation:

65 – 70% **Fats**

25 – 30% **Proteins**

5% **Carbohydrates**

But even though this may seem impossible to accomplish on daily basis, if you know which ingredients to use and which will only cause your weight to rise, the Ketogenic diet is pretty straightforward and easy plan to follow.

WHAT TO FOODS TO EAT AND FOODS TO AVOID

What to Eat

- Meat (fresh and processed meat)
- Seafood
- Eggs
- All Dairy Products (milk, cheeses, heavy cream, sour cream, yogurt, butter, etc.)
- Avocados (low in carbs, high in healthy fats)
- Non Starchy Veggies (broccoli, leafy greens, cauliflower, asparagus, Brussel sprouts, zucchini, cabbage, tomatoes, etc.)
- Lower-in-carbs Fruits (Berries, watermelon, citrus fruits, etc.)
- Seeds
- Nuts
- Oils (aim for the healthiest kind such as olive oil, coconut oil, flaxseed oil, etc.)

What to Avoid

- Grains
- Beans and Legumes
- Sugar

- Trans Fats

- Fruit Juices

- Starchy Veggies (corn, potatoes, peas, parsnips, etc.)

- Diet Soda

- Refined Gats and Oils (such as margarine)

How Can the Instant Pot Help?

If you own an Instant Pot, you are already familiar with everything that this revolutionary kitchen appliance can do. It works as a:

1. A Saute Pan

2. A Pressure Cooker

3. A Rice Cooker

4. A Steamer

5. A Slow Cooker

6. Warming Pot

7. A Yogurt Maker

It multiple buttons allow hassle-free cooking and it is kind of obvious that this is one extremely valuable gadget to have. But how can it help during your Ketogenic experience?

Since the Ketogenic diet is quite restrictive, it is of utmost importance that the nutrient intake is balanced. And what better way to ensure that than to cook your food in an Instant Pot? The Instant Pot will not cause your food to lose its vitamins and minerals during cooking, unlike the conventional cooking appliances. And besides ensuring proper nutrition, the Instant Pot also ensures quick cooking without sacrificing your free afternoon. Doesn't that sound like a good reason to give these yummy recipes a try?

THE INSTANT POT PRESSURE COOKER

Instant Pot is a great substitute to your Pressure Cooker, Slow Cooker, Rice Cooker, Steamer, Microwave and Yogurt Maker. It has 7 different functions in just 1 cooker. It has smart programs that is user-friendly because of its easy-to-use control panel.

It is as easy as pressing a button. You can now prepare a variety of food for your family.

Features

- It has 10 safety mechanisms and UL safety certification.

- Energy efficient and kitchen friendly.

- Manual setting up to 120 minutes of cook time

- Multi-functional features from braising, pressure cooking, stewing, steaming, simmering, slow cooking, sauté/browning, fermenting, making yogurt and warming up foods.

- Has microprocessor inside that control time, cooking temperature and pressure. It has 14 cooking programs.

- Meal planner because you can use the feature delayed cooking up to 24 hours.

- Efficient and effective design because it can preserve the flavor and aroma of your food.

This cooker has different multi-functions specially designed for your needs. Below are the controls that you can use with this pot. It is very easy to use and so efficient. You will save dozen of time using this Instant Pot.

Functions

- *Manual* – This key is to set the time manually depending on what you need. You can set it up to 240 minutes or 4 hours.

- *Keep Warm/Cancel* – This key is the standard standby state of the cooker. Press to cancel the cooking and/or activate the keep-warm function.

- *Meat/Stew* – This key is for red meats and stew cooking. Enjoy a meal full of vegetables or meat cooked slowly in its broth.

- *Poultry* – When you cook chicken, turkey, or other "white" meats, etc. Savor the flavor of your favorite poultry meal.

- **Soup** – This key is for soup and broth making. It is hassle-free and saves time a lot of time when preparing a delicious soup or broth.

- **Porridge** - This key is for making porridge using various grains such as oatmeal.

- **Delay/Timer** – This key is for delayed cooking. You can setup the time in the morning and schedule it in the afternoon so when you came home a meal will be ready for you

- **Rice** – This key is for cooking white rice. No more mixing of rice. Just measure the right amount of cup of rice and water and wait for it to cook.

- **Bean/Chili** – This key is for cooking beans and making chili. This is perfect for those who wants to take their beans in the next level.

- **Steam** – This key is designed for steaming vegetables or your side dish.

- **Multigrain** – This key is used for cooking other kind of rice like the brown rice and other grains like quinoa.

- **Slow Cook** – This key is used if you want to turn your instant pot to a conventional slow cooker. The user can change the cooking time by pressing the "+" or "-".

- **Yogurt** – This function fo the Instant Pot allows you to make yogurt, pasteurize mile and make fermented glutinous rice.

- **Sauté** – This key is used for sautéing, browning or simmering inside the inner pot, always with the lid off.

Most of the controls can be adjusted depending on your need. You can slow it down or make it faster to achieve the style or the taste that you are looking for.

If you are now excited to use your Instant Pot, it's time to explore the recipes provided for you. If you don't have an Instant Pot yet, get up now and buy one so you can get started in your kitchen!

Let's start cooking!

BREAKFAST RECIPES

Bacon & Sausage Omelet

Preparation time: 15 minutes | Cooking time: 25 minutes | Servings: 6

Ingredients:

1 Onion, diced
6 Eggs
6 Sausage Links, chopped
6 Bacon Slices, cooked and crumbled
½ cup Milk
¼ tsp dried Parsley
Salt and Pepper, to taste
1 ½ cups Water

Instructions:

Pour the water into the Instant Pot and lower the trivet. Crack the eggs open in a bowl and pour the milk over. Beat the eggs and milk along with some salt and pepper until well-incorporated and smooth. Stir in the parsley, onion, bacon, and sausage. Grab a baking dish and grease it with some cooking spray. Pour the egg mixture over. Place the baking dish on top of the trivet.

Close the lid of the Instant Pot and turn it clockwise to seal. Select the "MANUAL" cooking mode. Set the cooking time to 25 minutes. Cook on HIGH pressure.

When the timer goes off, press the "KEEP WARM/CANCEL" button. Release the pressure naturally by allowing the valve to drop down on its own. Open the lid carefully and remove the baking dish from the Instant Pot. Let the omelet cool completely.

Storing:

When cooled, slice the omelet into 6. Divide between airtight containers or Ziploc bags and refrigerate for up to 3 days. To freeze, transfer to Ziploc bags and freeze up to 3 months. Defrost in the microwave and microwave for a couple of minutes to enjoy.

Nutrition facts per serving:

Calories 220, Protein 17g, Total Carbs 2.8g, Net Carbs 2.5g, Total Fat 15g, Saturated Fat 9g, Fiber 0.3g, Sodium 350mg

Chili Egg Cubes

Preparation time: 10 minutes | Cooking time: 4 minutes | Servings: 6

Ingredients:

⅔ tsp Chili Powder
¼ tsp Sea Salt
¼ tsp Garlic Powder
6 Eggs
1 ½ cups Water

Instructions:

Grab a baking dish that can fit inside the Instant Pot and grease it with a little bit of cooking spray.

Crack the eggs into the dish and scramble them with a whisk. Sprinkle them with all the spices.

Pour the water into the Instant Pot and lower the trivet.

Place the baking dish on top of the trivet and put the lid on.

Turn it clockwise for a proper sealing. Select the "MANUAL" cooking mode and set the cooking time to 4 minutes. Cook on HIGH pressure.

When the timer goes off, press the "KEEP WARM/CANCEL" button.

Turn the pressure handle to "Venting" to release the pressure quickly and remove the dish from the Instant Pot.

Transfer the eggs to a cutting board and cut into cubes.

Storing:

Let the egg cubes cool completely and divide between 6 airtight containers. Place in the fridge for 4-5 days. To freeze, transfer to Ziploc bags and freeze up to 3 months. Defrost in the microwave and microwave for a couple of minutes to enjoy.

Nutrition facts per serving:

Calories 80, Protein 5g, Total Carbs 0g, Net Carbs 0g, Total Fat 4g, Saturated Fat 1g, Fiber 0g, Sodium 250mg

Basil-Flavored Spinach & Bacon Eggs

Preparation time: 10 minutes | Cooking time: 15 minutes | Servings: 4

Ingredients:

½ cup chopped Spinach
4 Bacon Slices, diced
2 tbsp chopped Basil
3 tbsp Heavy Cream
8 Eggs, beaten
Salt and Pepper, to taste
1 ½ cups Water

Instructions:

Turn the Instant Pot on and set it to "SAUTE". Add the bacon pieces and cook them until they become crispy, about 2-3 minutes.

Transfer the bacon to a bowl and stir in the rest of the ingredients, except the water.

Grab a dish that can fit inside the Instant Pot and grease it with some cooking spray. Pour the egg mixture into the dish. Pour the water into the Instant Pot and lower the trivet. Place the baking dish on top of the trivet.

Close the lid and turn it clockwise to seal. Click on "MANUAL" and set the cooking time to 8 minutes. Cook on HIGH pressure.

When the timer goes off, press the "KEEP WARM/CANCEL" button. Turn the pressure handle to "Venting" for a quick pressure release and open the lid carefully.

Let cool completely.

Storing:

Divide between airtight containers or Ziploc bags and refrigerate for up to 3 days. To freeze, transfer to 4 Ziploc bags and freeze up to 3 months. Defrost in the microwave and microwave for a couple of minutes to enjoy.

Nutrition facts per serving:

Calories 275, Protein g, Total Carbs 4.2 g, Net Carbs 2g, Total Fat 21g, Saturated Fat 8g, Fiber 2g, Sodium 310mg

Mexican Chili Eggs

Preparation time: 10 minutes | Cooking time: 20 minutes | Servings: 4

Ingredients:

1 cup shredded Cheddar or other matured Cheese
1 cup Heavy Cream
4 Eggs
⅓ cup chopped canned Chilies
2 tbsp chopped Cilantro
1 tbsp chopped Parsley
¼ tsp Garlic Powder
¼ tsp Onion Powder
¼ tsp Cumin
Salt and Pepper, to taste
1 ½ cups Water

Instructions:

Pour the water into your Instant Pot and lower the rack. In a bowl, beat the eggs and stir in the remaining ingredients. Grease a baking dish with some cooking spray and pour the egg mixture inside. Place the baking dish on top of the trivet.

Put the lid on and seal by turning clockwise. Select the "MANUAL" cooking mode. Set the cooking time to 20 minutes. Cook on HIGH pressure.

After the beep, press the "KEEP WARM/CANCEL" button. Release the pressure naturally by allowing the valve to drop down on its own. Open the lid and take the dish out. Cut into 4 pieces and serve. Let cool completely.

Storing:

Divide between 4 airtight containers. Place in the fridge for up to 3 days. To freeze, transfer to Ziploc bags and freeze up to 3 months. Defrost in the microwave and microwave for a couple of minutes to enjoy.

Nutrition facts per serving:

Calories 270, Protein 14g, Total Carbs 3.5g, Net Carbs 2.5g, Total Fat 19g, Saturated Fat 7.5g, Fiber 1g, Sodium 390mg

Very Berry Ricotta Pancakes

Preparation time: 10 minutes | Cooking time: 45 minutes | Servings: 4

Ingredients:

1 tbsp chopped Blackberries
2 tbsp Blueberries
1 tbsp mashed Strawberries
¾ cup Ricotta
3 Eggs
1 cup Almond Flour
¼ cup Milk
½ tsp Stevia
½ cup Flaxseed Meal
1 tsp Baking Powder
½ tsp Vanilla Extract
Pinch of Sea Salt
1 ½ cups Water

Instructions:

Pour the water into the Instant Pot and lower the trivet. Place the strawberry mash, ricotta, stevia, milk, eggs, and vanilla extract in a blender.

Blend the mixture until it becomes smooth. In a bowl, stir together the flaxseed meal, almond flour, baking powder, and salt. Stir the dry mixture into the wet one until the batter is smooth and well-incorporated. Finally, fold in the berries.

Grease a baking dish with some cooking spray and pour the pancake batter into it. Place the dish on top of the trivet and close the lid. Turn it clockwise for a proper sealing.

Select the "MANUAL" cooking mode and then set the cooking time to 45 minutes, but make sure to cook on LOW pressure. When the timer goes off, press the "KEEP WARM/CANCEL" button. Turn the pressure handle to "Venting" for a quick pressure release and open the lid carefully.

Remove the dish from the Instant Pot. Divide the pancake into 4 servings.

Storing:

When cooled, divide the pancake between 4 airtight containers. Enjoy for up to 4-6 days. To freeze, transfer to a container. Let set a little and put in the freezer. Divide between 4 Ziploc bags and arrange them in a single layer. When frozen, store them in the freezer as desired. The oatmeal will stay safe for up to 3-6 months in the freezer.

Nutrition facts per serving:

Calories 390, Protein 19g, Total Carbs 7g, Net Carbs 3.5g, Total Fat 24g, Saturated Fat 8g, Fiber 5.5g, Sodium 150mg

Basil and Parsley Scramble

Preparation time: 10 minutes | Cooking time: 5 minutes | Servings: 4

Ingredients:

8 Eggs
¼ cup chopped Parsley
3 tbsp chopped Basil
¼ tsp Garlic Powder
¼ tsp Salt
¼ tsp Pepper
¼ cup Milk
1 tbsp Butter

Instructions:

Turn the Instant Pot on and set it to "SAUTE".

Add the butter and let it melt. Meanwhile, beat the eggs in a bowl and stir in the remaining ingredients.

Pour the egg mixture into the Instant Pot and stir for about 5 minutes with a spatula, until the eggs are set.

You will not be bringing the Instant Pot to pressure so you don't need water.

Let cool completely.

Storing:

When cooled, place the eggs in an airtight container and in the fridge. You can use them for up to 7-10 days.

The egg whites are not freezer-friendly, but you can freeze the yolks for up to month or two.

Nutrition facts per serving:

Calories 295, Protein 12g, Total Carbs 3.2g, Net Carbs 2.2g, Total Fat 15g, Saturated Fat 4g, Fiber 1g, Sodium 420mg

Vanilla Cheesecake Pancakes

Preparation time: 5 minutes | Cooking time: 10 minutes | Servings: 4

Ingredients:

4 ounces Cream Cheese
½ tsp Vanilla Extract
4 tsp Butter
4 Eggs
1 tsp Granulated Sweetener
Pinch of Cinnamon, optional

Instructions:

Turn on your Instant Pot and set it to "SAUTE". In a blender, crack the eggs, cream cheese, sweetener, and cinnamon, if using. Blend until the mixture becomes smooth and well-combined.

In the Instant Pot, melt half of the butter. Add half of the pancake batter and cook for about 3 minutes. When set, flip the pancake over and cook for another 2 minutes.

Melt the remaining butter and repeat the same process with the remaining batter. You should have four fluffy and delicious cream cheese pancakes. Let cool completely.

Storing:

When cooled, place in an air-tight container or in a Ziploc bag; and put in the fridge. It is best to enjoy it up to 3 days from preparing. For freezing, put in Ziploc bag and place in the freezer. Defrost overnight in the fridge and microwave for a few minutes to enjoy.

Nutrition facts per serving:

Calories 345, Protein 17g, Total Carbs 3.5g, Net Carbs 2.5g, Total Fat 29g, Saturated Fat 11g, Fiber 1.5g, Sodium 50mg

SNACKS AND APPETIZERS

Cauliflower Tots

Preparation time: 10 minutes | Cooking time: 6 minutes | Servings: 4

Ingredients:

1 Cauliflower Head, chopped
1 ½ cups Water
⅓ cup shredded Cheddar Cheese
4 Egg Whites
2 tbsp Butter
2 tbsp Heavy Cream
Salt and Pepper, to taste

Instructions:

Pour the water into your Instant Pot. Place the cauliflower pieces inside the steamer basket and lower the basket into the pot. Put the lid on, turn it clockwise to seal, and hit the "MANUAL" button. With the help of the "+" and "-" buttons, set the cooking time to 3 minutes. Cook on HIGH pressure.

After the beep, select the "KEEP WARM/CANCEL" button. Turn the pressure handle to "Venting" for a quick pressure release and open the lid carefully. Place the cauliflower florets in a bowl and allow to cool. Discard the water and wipe the pot clean.

When the cauliflower is safe to handle, add the rest of the ingredients, except the butter, to the bowl. Mash the mixture until well pureed and wet your hands. Make small nuggets out of the mixture.

Melt the butter in the Instant Pot on "SAUTE" and add the nuggets to it. Cook them on both sides until they become golden, about a few minutes. Once ready, let cool before storing.

Storing:

When cooled, divide between 4 airtight containers. Place in the fridge. You can use them for up to 3 days. To freeze, divide among 4 Ziploc bags and place in the freezer for up to 3 months. Defrost in microwave and heat for a few minutes.

Nutrition facts per serving:

Calories 250, Protein 10g, Total Carbs 2.5g, Net Carbs 2g, Total Fat 21g, Saturated Fat 9g, Fiber 0.5g, Sodium 160mg

Mini Biscuits

Preparation time: 10 minutes | Cooking time: 10 minutes | Servings: 8

Ingredients:

½ cup Coconut Flour
2 small Eggs
¼ cup Butter
⅓ plus 2 tbsp Milk
1 tbsp Gluten-Free Baking Mix
Pinch of Xanthan Gum
½ tbsp Sugar-Free Vanilla Protein Powder
¼ tsp Salt
1 ½ cups Water

Instructions:

Pour the water into your Instant Pot and lower the trivet. Grease a baking tray that fits inside the Instant Pot and set it aside.

Place all of the dry ingredients in a bowl and stir to combine them well. Add the butter to the bowl and with your fingers, rub it into the mixture until a crumbly texture forms. Add the wet ingredients and stir well to combine the mixture. Lightly flour your working surface and transfer the dough there. With a rolling pin, roll out the dough. Cut into 8 small pieces and arrange the mini biscuits on the greased tray.

Place the tray on top of the trivet and close the lid. Turn it clockwise to seal and select "MANUAL". Cook on HIGH pressure for 10 minutes.

After the beep, select the "KEEP WARM/CANCEL" button. Turn the pressure handle to "Venting" for a quick pressure release and open the lid carefully.

Storing:

Divide between 8 airtight containers and place in the fridge. You can use them for up to 3 days. To freeze, transfer the dip to an ice cube tray. To consume, thaw it in the fridge overnight and serve cold.

Nutrition facts per serving:

Calories 100, Protein 2.5g, Total Carbs 3g, Net Carbs 2g, Total Fat 8g, Saturated Fat 1.5g, Fiber 1g, Sodium 85mg

Stuffed Mini Peppers

Preparation time: 10 minutes | Cooking time: 2 minutes | Servings: 4

Ingredients:

8 canned Piquillo Peppers
1 ½ Prosciutto Slices, cut into 8 pieces in total
½ tbsp Olive Oil
½ tbsp Balsamic Vinegar
1 ½ cups Water

Filling:

1 ½ tbsp Heavy Cream
½ cup grated Mozzarella Cheese
1 tbsp chopped Parsley
½ tbsp Olive Oil
Pinch of each Garlic and Onion Powder

Instructions:

Pour the water into your Instant Pot and lower the trivet. Place all of the filling ingredients in a bowl and mix to combine everything well. Stuff the peppers with the filling and then arrange them on a greased baking dish. Place the dish on top of the trivet and close the lid of the Instant Pot. Seal by turning the lid clockwise. Select "MANUAL" and set the cooking time to 2 minutes. Cook on HIGH pressure. The point is for the cheese to be melted and the peppers to be soft.

When the timer goes off, choose "KEEP WARM/CANCEL". Turn the pressure handle to "Venting" for a quick pressure release and open the lid carefully. Arrange the stuffed peppers on a platter and drizzle with the olive oil and balsamic vinegar.

Storing:

When cooled, divide between 4 airtight containers and place in the fridge. You can use them for up to 3 days. To freeze, divide among 4 Ziploc bags and place in the freezer for up to 3 months. Defrost in the fridge overnight and heat for a few minutes.

Nutrition facts per serving:

Calories 110, Protein 6g, Total Carbs 4.5g, Net Carbs 2.5g, Total Fat 9g, Saturated Fat 1.5g, Fiber 2g, Sodium 160mg

Gorgonzola Chicken Dip

Preparation time: 10 minutes | Cooking time: 4 minutes | Servings: 8

Ingredients:

½ cup Gorgonzola Dressing
1 ½ cups cooked and shredded Chicken
¼ cup shredded Mozzarella Cheese
2 tbsp grated Parmesan Cheese

2 tbsp Hot Sauce
8 ounces Cream Cheese
1 ½ cups Water

Instructions:

Pour the water into your Instant Pot and lower the trivet. Place all of the ingredients in a baking dish and stir well to combine. Place the baking dish on top of the trivet and close the lid.

Turn it clockwise to seal properly. Select "MANUAL" and set the cooking time to 4 minutes. Cook on HIGH pressure. After the beep, select the "KEEP WARM/CANCEL" button. Turn the pressure handle to "Venting" for a quick pressure release and open the lid carefully.

Storing:

When cooled, divide between 8 airtight containers and add other snacks alongside. Place in the fridge. Use up to 5 days. To freeze, divide among 4 Ziploc bags and place in the freezer for up to 3 months. Defrost in microwave and heat for a few minutes.

Nutrition facts per serving:

Calories 110, Protein 8g, Total Carbs 1g, Net Carbs 1g, Total Fat 10g, Saturated Fat 3.4g, Fiber 0g, Sodium 150mg

Caulicheese Mini Bowls

Preparation time: 10 minutes | Cooking time: 5 minutes | Servings: 4

Ingredients:

½ cup Half & Half
2 cups Cauliflower Rice
2 tbsp Cream Cheese

½ cup shredded Cheddar Cheese
Salt and Pepper, to taste
1 ½ cups Water

Instructions:

Pour the water into the Instant Pot and lower the trivet. Place all of the remaining ingredients in a baking dish. Stir to combine well and season the mixture with salt and pepper, to taste. Place the baking dish on top of the trivet and close the lid.

Seal by turning the lid clockwise. Select "MANUAL" and set the cooking time to 5 minutes. Cook on HIGH pressure.

After the beeping sound, select the "KEEP WARM/CANCEL" button. Allow the pressure valve to drop on its own for a natural pressure release.

Storing:

When cooled, divide between airtight containers and place in the fridge. Consume within 2-3 days. To freeze, divide among 4 Ziploc bags and place in the freezer for up to 2-3 months. Defrost overnight in the fridge, and heat in the microwave.

Nutrition facts per serving:

Calories 134, Protein 5g, Total Carbs 4g, Net Carbs 2.5g, Total Fat 10g, Saturated Fat 2g, Fiber 1g, Sodium 185mg

Zucchini Ham and Cheese Rolls

Preparation time: 7 minutes | Cooking time: 3 minutes | Servings: 4

Ingredients:

4 Zucchini Slices (Sliced Lengthwise)
4 Ham Slices

⅓ cup grated Cheddar Cheese
1 tbsp Butter

Instructions:

Set your Instant Pot to "SAUTE" and add the butter to it. While the pot is getting heated, prepare the rolls. Lay out the zucchini slices on a working surface. Arrange a ham slice over and sprinkle with the cheese on top. Roll them up carefully and secure with toothpicks.

When the butter is melted, place the zucchini rolls inside your Instant Pot. Cook them for about 2-3 minutes, until the zucchinis are browned and the cheese is melted. Allow to cool.

Storing:

When cooled, divide between 4 airtight containers. You can add some cream cheese, hummus, or other dip and veggies to the container, if desired. Place in the fridge. You can use them for up to 3 days. To freeze, divide among 4 Ziploc bags and place in the freezer for up to 3 months. Defrost in the fridge overnight and heat in the microwave before consuming.

Nutrition facts per serving:

Calories 70, Protein 3g, Total Carbs 1g, Net Carbs 1g, Total Fat 6g, Saturated Fat 1g, Fiber 0g, Sodium 75mg

Chili Party Meatballs

Preparation time: 10 minutes | Cooking time: 10 minutes | Servings: 4

Ingredients:

½ pound ground Beef
1 small Egg
2 tbsp grated Parmesan Cheese
2 tbsp Hot Sauce
½ tsp Chili Powder
¼ tsp Garlic Powder
¼ tsp Onion Powder
1 tbsp Olive Oil
1 ½ cup Water

Instructions:

Set your Instant Pot to "SAUTE" and add the oil to it. While heating, prepare the meatballs by mixing all of the ingredients together, except the water, in a bowl. Mix with your hands until the mixture is well combined and then shape into meatballs.

When the oil is hot and sizzling, add the meatballs and cook for about 2 minutes per side, or until slightly browned.

Transfer to a greased baking dish and pour the water into the Instant Pot. Lower the trivet of the Instant Pot and place the dish on top of it. Put the lid on and turn it clockwise to seal. Select "MANUAL" and set the cooking time to 6 minutes. Cook on HIGH pressure.

After the beep, select the "KEEP WARM/CANCEL" button. Do a quick pressure release by turning the pressure handle to "Venting". Let cool completely.

Storing:

When cooled, divide between 4 small glass jars. Place in the fridge. You can use them for up to 2 days. To freeze, divide among 4 Ziploc bags and place in the freezer for up to 3 months. Defrost in microwave and heat for a few minutes.

Nutrition facts per serving:

Calories 140, Protein 13g, Total Carbs 1g, Net Carbs 1g, Total Fat 10g, Saturated Fat 2g, Fiber 0g, Sodium 290mg

Broccoli & Cheddar Nuggets

Preparation time: 10 minutes | Cooking time: 10 minutes | Servings: 4

Ingredients:

2 Egg Whites
1 cup shredded Cheese
¼ cup Almond Flour
2 cups Broccoli Florets
Salt and Pepper, to taste
1 ½ cups Water

Instructions:

Pour the water into the Instant Pot and lower the trivet. Place the broccoli inside the steamer basket and then lower the basket into the pot.

Close and seal the lid by turning it clockwise. Select "STEAM" and set the cooking time to 4 minutes. Cook on HIGH pressure.

After the beep, select the "KEEP WARM/CANCEL" button. Turn the pressure handle to "Venting" for a quick pressure release and open the lid carefully.

Transfer the broccoli to a bowl and mash them up with a potato masher. Add the rest of the ingredients and stir to combine well.

Line a baking sheet with parchment paper and then arrange scoops of the broccoli and cheese mixture onto the dish. Place the dish on top of the trivet.

Close and seal the lid again. Select "MANUAL" and cook on HIGH for 6 minutes.

Do a quick pressure release again let cool completely.

Storing:

When cooled, divide among 4 airtight containers. Place in the fridge. You can use them for up to 3 days. To freeze, divide among 4 Ziploc bags and place in the freezer for up to 3 months. Defrost in microwave and heat for a few minutes.

Nutrition facts per serving:

Calories 140, Protein 10g, Total Carbs 5g, Net Carbs 4g, Total Fat 9g, Saturated Fat 3g, Fiber 1g, Sodium 120mg

Cauliflower Alfredo Dip

Preparation time: 10 minutes | Cooking time: 8 minutes | Servings: 4

Ingredients:

1 ½ cup Cauliflower Florets
¼ cup Heavy Cream
2 tbsp Butter
Pinch of Nutmeg
Salt and Pepper, to taste
2 tbsp grated Parmesan Cheese
1 ½ cups Water

Instructions:

Pour the water into your Instant Pot.

Place the cauliflower florets inside the steamer basket and lower the basket into the pot.

Put the lid on and turn it clockwise to seal. Select "STEAM" and set the cooking time to 4 minutes. Cook on HIGH pressure.

After the beep, press the "KEEP WARM/CANCEL" button.

Turn the pressure handle to "Venting" for a quick pressure release and open the lid carefully.

Transfer the cauliflower florets to a bowl and mash them with a potato masher until well pureed.

Add the rest of the ingredients and mix everything well.

Let cool completely before storing.

Storing:

When cooled, divide between 4 airtight containers. Place in the fridge. You can use them for up to 4-6 days. To freeze, divide among 4 Ziploc bags and place in the freezer for up to 3 months. Defrost in the fridge overnight and heat for a few minutes.

Nutrition facts per serving:

Calories 105, Protein 4g, Total Carbs 2g, Net Carbs 1.5g, Total Fat 8g, Saturated Fat 2g, Fiber 0.5g, Sodium 95mg

Veggie Tomato Dip

Preparation time: 10 minutes | Cooking time: 11 minutes | Servings: 8

Ingredients:

1 cup chopped Broccoli
1 cup chopped Cauliflower
¼ Onion, diced
1 cup diced canned Tomatoes
1 tbsp Butter
¼ cup shredded Cheddar Cheese
¼ tsp Garlic Powder
Salt and Pepper, to taste
1 ½ cups Water

Instructions:

Pour the water into your Instant Pot. Place the cauliflower and broccoli inside the steamer basket and lower them into the pot. Put the lid on and turn it clockwise to seal. After you hear the chime, select "MANUAL" and set the cooking time to 4 minutes. Cook on HIGH pressure.

When the IP reads 00:00, select the "KEEP WARM/CANCEL" button. Move the pressure handle to "Venting" for a quick pressure release and open the lid carefully. Transfer the veggies to a bowl and mash them finely with a potato masher. Discard the water from the Instant Pot and wipe the pot clean.

Set the Instant Pot to "SAUTE" and met the butter in it. Add the onions and cook for about 3 minutes. When softened, add the tomatoes and spices and cook for 2 minutes. Stir in the mashed veggies and cheese, and cook for another 2 minutes. Let cool completely before storing.

Storing:

When cooled, divide among airtight containers. Place in the fridge. You can use them for up to 4-6 days. To freeze, divide among 4 Ziploc bags and place in the freezer for up to 3 months. Defrost in the fridge overnight.

Nutrition facts per serving:

Calories 120, Protein 4g, Total Carbs 5g, Net Carbs 4g, Total Fat 5g, Saturated Fat 1g, Fiber 1g, Sodium 142mg

Cream Cheese & Salami Snack

Preparation time: 10 minutes | Cooking time: 3 minutes | Servings: 6

Ingredients:

4 ounces Cream Cheese
¼ cup chopped Parsley

7 ounces dried Salami
1 cup Water

Instructions:

Pour the water into the Instant Pot and lower the trivet. Grab a baking sheet that fits inside the Instant Pot and arrange the salami slices on it. Place the baking sheet on top of the trivet and close the lid of the pot. Select "MANUAL" and set the cooking time to 3 minutes. Cook on HIGH pressure.

When the Instant Pot reads 00:00, select the "KEEP WARM/CANCEL" button. Move the handle from "Sealing" to "Venting" for a quick pressure release and open the lid carefully. Transfer the salami to a platter and top with some cream cheese. Sprinkle the parsley on top. Let cool before storing.

Storing:

When cooled, divide between 6 airtight containers. Place in the fridge. You can use them for up to 3-4 days. To freeze, divide among 4 Ziploc bags and place in the freezer for up to 3 months. Defrost in microwave and heat for a few minutes.

Nutrition facts per serving:

Calories 120, Protein 9g, Total Carbs 1g, Net Carbs 1g, Total Fat 15g, Saturated Fat 8g, Fiber 0g, Sodium 175mg

Mini Haddock Bites

Preparation time: 10 minutes | Cooking time: 5 minutes | Servings: 4

Ingredients:

1 pound Haddock, chopped
3 Eggs
Juice of 1 Lemon
½ cup Half and Half
3 tbsp Olive Oil

1 tsp Coriander
2 tbsp ground Almonds
1 tsp Lemon Zest
Pinch of Pepper

Instructions:

In a bowl, whisk together the eggs, flour, zest, and spices. Set your Instant Pot to "SAUTE" and add the oil to it. Dip the haddock pieces in egg mixture and then place in the IP to fry.

Cook for about a minute per side, or until golden. Pour the half and half and lemon juice over and stir to combine. Put the lid on and turn it clockwise to seal. Select "MANUAL" and set the cooking time to 2 minutes. Cook on HIGH pressure. After the beep, hit "KEEP WARM/CANCEL". Turn the pressure handle to "Venting" for a quick pressure release and open the lid carefully. Let cool before storing.

Storing:

When cooled, divide among 4 airtight containers. Place in the fridge. You can use them for up to 3 days. To freeze, divide among 4 Ziploc bags and place in the freezer for up to 3 months. Defrost in microwave and heat for a few minutes.

Nutrition facts per serving:

Calories 160, Protein 15g, Total Carbs 2.3g, Net Carbs 2.3g, Total Fat 10g, Saturated Fat 4g, Fiber 0g, Sodium 150mg

Prosciutto Wrapped Chicken Sticks

Preparation time: 10 minutes | Cooking time: 10 minutes | Servings: 4

Ingredients:

8 Strips of Provolone Cheese

8 Prosciutto Slices

12 ounces Chicken Tenders

Instructions:

Pound the chicken with a meat pounder until the meat becomes about ½-inch thick. Then cut it into 8 equal pieces. Place a provolone strip on top of each chicken stick and wrap them together with a prosciutto slice.

Set your Instant Pot to "SAUTE" and add the chicken wraps inside. Cook them for about 4 minutes per side, or until the chicken is no longer pink in the middle (Run a knife through the meat to check). Let cool before storing.

Storing:

When cooled, divide among 4 airtight containers. Place in the fridge. You can use them for up to 2 days. To freeze, divide among 4 Ziploc bags and place in the freezer for up to 3 months. Defrost in microwave and heat for a few minutes.

Nutrition facts per serving:

Calories 125, Protein 12g, Total Carbs 1.7g, Net Carbs 0.7g, Total Fat 15g, Saturated Fat 9.2g, Fiber 1g, Sodium 180mg

Green Devilled Eggs

Preparation time: 10 minutes | Cooking time: 10 minutes | Servings: 4

Ingredients:

1 ½ tbsp Green Tabasco
⅓ cup Mayonnaise
Salt and Pepper, to taste
1 cup Water

Instructions:

Pour the water into the Instant Pot. Place the eggs inside the steamer basket and lower it into the pot.

Close and seal the lid by turning it clockwise and then select the "MANUAL" cooking mode.

Set the cooking time to 7 minutes and cook on HIGH pressure.

After the beep, select the "KEEP WARM/CANCEL" button.

Turn the pressure handle to "Venting" for a quick pressure release and open the lid carefully.

Prepare an ice bath and drop the eggs into it, so you can speed up the cooling process.

When safe to handle, peel the eggs.

Cut the eggs in half and scoop out the yolks.

Place the yolks in a bowl along with the remaining ingredients.

Mix to combine well and then fill the egg holes with the yolk/tabasco mixture.

Let cool completely.

Storing:

Divide among 4 airtight containers. Place in the fridge. You can use them for up to 3 days. To freeze, divide among 4 Ziploc bags and place in the freezer for up to 3 months. Defrost in the fridge overnight and warm microwave them for a couple of minutes.

Nutrition facts per serving:

Calories 150, Protein 6g, Total Carbs 4g, Net Carbs 3g, Total Fat 15g, Saturated Fat 11g, Fiber 1g, Sodium 220mg

Chicken Ranch Dip

Preparation time: 10 minutes | Cooking time: 10 minutes | Servings: 4

Ingredients:

1 pound Chicken Breasts

16 ounces shredded Cheddar Cheese

1 cup Hot Sauce

1 packet Ranch Seasoning

1 Stick of Butter

8 ounces of Cream Cheese

Salt and Pepper, to taste

Instructions:

Place all of the ingredients in your Instant Pot and give the mixture a stir to combine.

Put the lid on and turn it clockwise to seal.

Select "MANUAL" and set the cooking time to 15 minutes. Make sure to cook on HIGH pressure.

After the alarm goes off, select the "KEEP WARM/CANCEL" button.

Turn the pressure handle from "Sealing" to "Venting" to release the pressure quickly, and open the lid carefully.

Grab two forks and shred the chicken within the pot, well.

Let cool completely before storing.

Storing:

When cooled, divide between 4 airtight containers. Place in the fridge. You can use them for up to 3 days. To freeze, divide among 4 small Ziploc bags and place in the freezer for up to 3 months. Defrost in microwave and heat for a few minutes.

Nutrition facts per serving:

Calories 110, Protein 11g, Total Carbs 1g, Net Carbs 1g, Total Fat 15g, Saturated Fat 6g, Fiber 0g, Sodium 180mg

POULTRY RECIPES

Chicken Meatballs with Parmesan

Preparation time: 10 minutes | Cooking time: 15 minutes | Servings: 4

Ingredients:

Ingredients:
1 pound ground Chicken Meat
½ Onion, grated
½ cup Almond Flour
¼ cup grated Parmesan Cheese
¼ cup Salsa or Tomato Sauce
1 Egg
Salt and Pepper, to taste

Instructions:

Pour the water into the Instant Pot and lower the trivet. Place all of the remaining ingredients in a large bowl and mix with your hands until well combined.

Shape the mixture into meatballs and arrange on a previously greased baking dish that can fit inside the Instant Pot. Place the baking dish on top of the trivet and put the lid on.

Turn clockwise to seal. Hit "MANUAL" and set the cooking time to 15 minutes. Cook on HIGH pressure.

After the beep, press the "KEEP WARM/CANCEL" button. Turn the pressure handle from "Sealing" to "Venting" for a quick pressure release and open the lid carefully. Let cool completely before storing.

Storing:

When cooled, divide between 4 airtight containers. Place in the fridge. You can use them for up to 3 days. To freeze, divide among 4 Ziploc bags and place in the freezer for up to 3 months. Defrost in microwave and heat for a few minutes.

Nutrition facts per serving:

Calories 220, Protein 22g, Total Carbs 3g, Net Carbs 2g, Total Fat 12g, Saturated Fat 5g, Fiber 1g, Sodium 350mg

Jalapeno and Cheddar Chicken

Preparation time: 10 minutes | Cooking time: 12 minutes | Servings: 4

Ingredients:

Ingredients:
1 pound Chicken Breasts
8 ounces Cream Cheese
8 ounces shredded Cheddar Cheese
3 Jalapenos, seeded and diced
½ cup Water
7 ounces Sour Cream
Salt and Pepper, to taste

Instructions:

Place the water, cream cheese, and sour cream, inside the Instant Pot.

Whisk until the mixture is combined. Stir in the jalapenos and cheddar.

Place the chicken inside and put the lid on. Turn the lid clockwise to seal. After the chime, hit the "MANUAL" button.

Set the cooking time to 12 minutes and cook on HIGH pressure.

When the timer goes off, press the "KEEP WARM/CANCEL" button.

Turn the pressure handle to "Venting" for a quick pressure release and open the lid carefully.

Shred the chicken with two forks and stir to combine.

Let sit until completely cooled.

Storing:

When cooled, divide between 4 airtight containers. Place in the fridge. You can use them for up to 3 days. To freeze, divide among 4 Ziploc bags and place in the freezer for up to 3 months. Defrost the chicken in your microwave and heat for a few minutes to enjoy warm.

Nutrition facts per serving:

Calories 310, Protein 20g, Total Carbs 4.4g, Net Carbs 3g, Total Fat 25g, Saturated Fat 13g, Fiber 1.4g, Sodium 350mg

Cream Cheese Chicken with Tomatoes and Zucchini

Preparation time: 10 minutes | Cooking time: 25 minutes | Servings: 4

Ingredients:

1 cup Cream Cheese
1 cup Tomato Sauce
2 Tomatoes, peeled and diced
1 cup shredded Zucchini
1 ½ cup Chicken Broth
½ tsp Garlic Powder
1 pound Chicken, cut into 4 fillets
Salt and Pepper, to taste

Instructions:

Pour the chicken broth inside the Instant Pot and place the chicken inside.

Put the lid on and turn it clockwise for a proper sealing.

Select "MANUAL" and set the cooking time to 20 minutes. Cook on HIGH pressure.

When you hear the beep, select the "KEEP WARM/CANCEL" button.

Turn the pressure handle to "Venting" for a quick pressure release and open the lid carefully. Stir in all of the remaining ingredients.

Seal the lid again and cook for additional 5 minutes on HIGH.

Again, do a quick pressure release. Allow to cool before storing.

Storing:

When cooled, divide between 4 airtight containers or Ziploc bags. Place in the fridge. You can enjoy the chicken for up to 3 days. To freeze, divide among 4 Ziploc bags and place in the freezer for up to 3 months. Defrost in microwave and heat for a few minutes.

Nutrition facts per serving:

Calories 260, Protein 28g, Total Carbs 4g, Net Carbs 2.5g, Total Fat 19g, Saturated Fat 11g, Fiber 1.5g, Sodium 400mg

Tomato and Coconut Chicken

Preparation time: 10 minutes | Cooking time: 20 minutes | Servings: 4

Ingredients:

1 Onion, diced
1 pound Chicken Breasts, cubed
1 cup Coconut Cream
1 tsp minced Garlic
3 tbsp Butter
1 14-ounce can diced Tomatoes, undrained
¼ cup Chicken Broth
Salt and Pepper, to taste

Instructions:

Set your Instant Pot to "SAUTE" and add the butter to it. When melted, add the onions and cook for about 3-4 minutes. When softened, stir in the garlic and cook for one more minute. Stir in the chicken and tomatoes and season with salt and pepper.

Pour the broth over and close the lid. Turn it clockwise for a proper sealing.

Select "MANUAL" and set the cooking time to 15 minutes. Cook on HIGH pressure.

When the timer goes off, hit "KEEP WARM/CANCEL". Turn the handle to "Venting" to release the pressure all at once.

Open the lid gently and stir in the coconut cream. Taste and season with some more salt and pepper if needed.

Let the chicken cool completely.

Storing:

When cooled, divide among 4 airtight containers and place in the fridge. Consume within 3 days. To freeze, divide among 4 Ziploc bags and place in the freezer for up to 3 months. Defrost in the microwave or in the fridge overnight and heat for a few minutes in order to consume warm.

Nutrition facts per serving:

Calories 410, Protein 38g, Total Carbs 4g, Net Carbs 2g, Total Fat 40g, Saturated Fat 15g, Fiber 2g, Sodium 500mg

Curried Chicken Patties

Preparation time: 10 minutes | Cooking time: 13 minutes | Servings: 4

Ingredients:

1 Egg
¼ cup grated Parmesan Cheese
1 pound Ground Chicken
1 tbsp chopped Parsley
¼ cup Cauliflower Rice
1 tsp Curry Powder
Salt and Pepper, to taste
2 tbsp Olive Oil
1 ½ cups Water

Instructions:

Pour the water into your Instant Pot and lower the trivet. Grease a baking dish that fits inside the Instant Pot with some cooking spray, and set aside.

Place the chicken, egg, curry powder, parsley, cauliflower, and parmesan in a large bowl. Season with some salt and pepper and mix the mixture with your hands. Shape the mixture into 4 patties and arrange them in the baking dish. Place the dish on top of the trivet and close the lid. Turn it clockwise to seal and then hit the "MANUAL" button. Cook for 10 minutes on HIGH.

When the Instant Pot reads 00:00, press the "KEEP WARM/CANCEL" button. Turn the pressure handle to "Venting" for a quick pressure release and open the lid carefully. Set the baking dish aside an discard the water. Wipe the pot clean. Set the Instant Pot to "SAUTE" and add half of the oil to it. When hot, place 2 patties inside. Cook for about 2 minutes per side, until golden. Repeat with the remaining oil and patties.

Let cool completely before storing.

Storing:

When cooled, divide between 4 airtight containers. Place in the fridge and consume within 3 days. Simply heat in the microwave. To freeze, transfer the chicken to 4 Ziploc bags and place in the freezer. Freeze for up to 3 months. Defrost in the fridge overnight and heat for a few minutes.

Nutrition facts per serving:

Calories 220, Protein 25g, Total Carbs 4g, Net Carbs 2g, Total Fat 19g, Saturated Fat 11g, Fiber 2g, Sodium 405mg

Mexican Chicken

Preparation time: 10 minutes | Cooking time: 15 minutes | Servings: 4

Ingredients:

1 Egg
1 pound Chicken Breasts, boneless and skinless
¾ tsp Cumin
1 Jalapeno, seeded and diced
1 cup mild Salsa or Tomato Sauce
½ tsp Onion Powder
¼ tsp Garlic Powder
1 cup Sour Cream
Pinch of Smoked Paprika
Salt and Pepper, to taste

Instructions:

Whisk together the salsa and sour cream inside the Instant Pot. Stir in the jalapeno and all of the spices. Place the chicken inside and close the lid.

Seal the pot by turning the lid clockwise. Select "MANUAL" and set the cooking time to 15 minutes. Cook on HIGH pressure.

When the timer goes off, press the "KEEP WARM/CANCEL" button. Turn the pressure handle to "Venting" for a quick pressure release and open the lid carefully. Grab two forks and shred the chicken inside the pot. Give it a good stir until the meat is combined with the sauce well.

Let cool completely before storing.

Storing:

When cooled, divide between 4 airtight containers. Place in the fridge and consume within 3 days. Simply heat in the microwave. To freeze, transfer the chicken to 4 Ziploc bags and place in the freezer. Freeze for up to 3 months. Defrost in the fridge overnight and heat for a few minutes.

Nutrition facts per serving:

Calories 250, Protein 29g, Total Carbs 5g, Net Carbs 2g, Total Fat 21g, Saturated Fat 13g, Fiber 3g, Sodium 385mg

Sour Cream Chicken with Cauliflower

Preparation time: 10 minutes | Cooking time: 15 minutes | Servings: 4

Ingredients:

4 Chicken Breasts, chopped

4 tbsp Butter

1 cup Chicken Broth

1 cup Sour Cream

½ Cauliflower Head, broken into florets

1 tsp minced Garlic

Instructions:

Set your Instant Pot to "SAUTE" and add the butter to it. When melted, whish in the broth and sour cream. Stir in the remaining ingredients and put the lid on. Turn the lid clockwise for a proper sealing. Select "MANUAL" and set the cooking time to 15 minutes. Cook on HIGH pressure.

When the timer goes off, press the "KEEP WARM/CANCEL" button. Release the pressure quickly by moving the handle from "Sealing" to "Venting". Open the lid carefully and stir to combine well.

Storing:

When cooled, divide between 4 airtight containers. Make sure to divide the sauce as well. Place in the fridge. Use for up to 3 days. To freeze, divide among 4 Ziploc bags and place in the freezer for up to 3 months. Defrost in the fridge overnight and heat for a few minutes in the microwave.

Nutrition facts per serving:

Calories 580, Protein 35g, Total Carbs 4g, Net Carbs 2.5g, Total Fat 35g, Saturated Fat 15g, Fiber 2.5g, Sodium 280mg

Greek Chicken Casserole

Preparation time: 10 minutes | Cooking time: 15 minutes | Servings: 4

Ingredients:

1 pound Chicken Breasts, chopped

½ cup sliced Kalamata Olives

1 cup halved Cherry Tomatoes

1 cup Cauliflower Rice

1 tbsp chopped Basil

1 tsp chopped Oregano

1 cup Chicken Broth

1 cup Sour Cream or Cream Cheese

Salt and Pepper, to taste

Instructions:

Dump all of the ingredients in your Instant Pot. Give the mixture a good stir until fully incorporated. Put the lid on and turn it clockwise to seal.

After the chime, select the "MANUAL" cooking mode and set the cooking time to 15 minutes. Cook on HIGH pressure. When you hear the beep, press the "KEEP WARM/CANCEL" button. Release the pressure quickly by moving the pressure handle to "Venting". Make sure to be careful when opening the lid. Let the chicken cool completely before storing.

Storing:

When cooled, divide between 4 airtight containers. Place in the fridge. Consume within 3 days. To freeze, divide among 4 Ziploc bags and place in the freezer in a single layer. When frozen, stack as desired. The chicken is safe to consume for up to 3 months. Defrost in microwave and heat for a few minutes.

Nutrition facts per serving:

Calories 380, Protein 35g, Total Carbs 5g, Net Carbs 2.5g, Total Fat 35g, Saturated Fat 17g, Fiber 3.5g, Sodium 325mg

Easy and Cheesy Chicken and Cauliflower

Preparation time: 5 minutes | Cooking time: 5 minutes | Servings: 4

Ingredients:

2 ½ cups cooked and shredded Chicken
½ cup Half and Half
2 cups chopped Cauliflower
½ cup shredded Mozzarella Cheese

½ cup Chicken Broth
¼ tsp Garlic Powder
Pinch of Onion Powder
Salt and Pepper, to taste

Instructions:

Place all of the ingredients in your Instant Pot. Stir well to combine everything and close the lid. Turn it clockwise for a proper sealing. Select "MANUAL" and set the cooking time to 2 minutes. Cook on HIGH pressure.

When the timer goes off, press the "KEEP WARM/CANCEL" button. Turn the pressure handle to "Venting" for a quick pressure release and open the lid carefully. Set the Instant Pot to "SAUTE". Cook for 2-3 additional minutes with the lid off. Let cool completely before storing.

Storing:

When cooled, divide between 4 airtight containers. Place in the fridge and consume within 3 days. To freeze, divide among 4 Ziploc bags and place in the freezer for up to 3 months. Defrost in the fridge overnight and heat in your microwave for a few minutes.

Nutrition facts per serving:

Calories 340, Protein 30g, Total Carbs 4g, Net Carbs 2.5g, Total Fat 25g, Saturated Fat 11g, Fiber 1.5g, Sodium 340mg

Chicken Thighs with Bacon and Cheese

Preparation time: 10 minutes | Cooking time: 20 minutes | Servings: 4

Ingredients:

4 Chicken Thighs
8 ounces Cream Cheese
½ cup shredded Cheddar Cheese
5 Bacon Slices, cooked and crumbled
¼ tsp Garlic Powder
¼ tsp Italian Seasoning
Salt and Pepper, to taste
1 cup Chicken Broth
2 tbsp Arrowroot

Instructions:

Whisk together the chicken broth, cream cheese, and all of the seasonings. Place the chicken thighs inside and put the lid on.

Turn it clockwise for a proper sealing. Select "MANUAL" and set the cooking time to 18 minutes. Cook on HIGH pressure.

When you hear the beep, press "KEEP WARM/CANCEL". Turn the pressure handle to "Venting" for a quick pressure release and open the lid carefully. Transfer the thighs to a plate and set the Instant Pot to "SAUTE". Whisk in the arrowroot and cook for about 2 minutes, or until the sauce thickens.

Let cool completely before storing.

Storing:

When cooled, divide between 4 airtight containers. Place in the fridge and consume within 3 days. Simply heat in the microwave. To freeze, transfer the chicken to 4 Ziploc bags and place in the freezer. Freeze for up to 3 months. Defrost in the fridge overnight and heat for a few minutes.

Nutrition facts per serving:

Calories 420, Protein 40g, Total Carbs 5g, Net Carbs 2.5g, Total Fat 45g, Saturated Fat 28g, Fiber 2.5g, Sodium 620mg

Hot Chicken Stew

Preparation time: 10 minutes | Cooking time: 15 minutes | Servings: 4

Ingredients:

1 ½ cups Chicken Broth
⅓ cup Hot Sauce
½ Onion, diced
2 Garlic Cloves, minced
1 Jalapeno, seeded and diced
1 cup Heavy Cream or Half & Half
2 cups shredded Cheddar Cheese
2 Chicken Breasts
2 tbsp Butter
1 Celery Stalk, diced
½ cup chopped Cauliflower Florets
Salt and Pepper, to taste

Instructions:

Place everything but the cream and cheese inside your Instant Pot. Give the mixture a good stir to combine and put the lid on. Turn the lid clockwise to seal the pot properly. After you hear the chime, press the "MANUAL" button. Set the cooking time to 15 minutes and make sure that the pressure is set to HIGH.

When the timer goes off, press the "KEEP WARM/CANCEL" button. Turn the pressure handle to "Venting" for a quick pressure release and open the lid carefully. Stir in the heavy cream (or Half & Half if using) and the cheese.

Let cool completely before storing.

Storing:

When cooled, divide between 4 airtight containers. Place in the fridge and consume within 3 days. Simply heat in the microwave. To freeze, transfer the chicken stew to 4 Ziploc bags and place in the freezer. Freeze for up to 3 months. Defrost in the fridge overnight and heat for a few minutes.

Nutrition facts per serving:

Calories 490, Protein 42g, Total Carbs 3g, Net Carbs 2.7g, Total Fat 35g, Saturated Fat 22g, Fiber 1.3g, Sodium 480 mg

Ranch and Lemon Whole Chicken

Preparation time: 10 minutes | Cooking time: 30 minutes | Servings: 6

Ingredients:

1 Chicken (medium size)
1 ½ cups Chicken Broth
1 Onion, quartered
1 ½ tsp Ranch Seasoning
½ tsp Lemon Pepper
1 Lemon, halved
1 Thyme Sprig
1 Rosemary Sprig
2 Garlic Cloves
1 tbsp Butter

Instructions:

Set your Instant Pot to "SAUTE". Wash the chicken well and pat it dry with some paper towels. In a small bowl combine the Ranch seasoning and lemon pepper and rub the seasoning into the chicken. Add the butter to the Instant Pot and when it is melted, sear the chicken on all sides, until golden. Stuff the chicken's cavity with lemon, onion, garlic, thyme, and rosemary.

Place the chicken inside the Instant Pot and pour the broth around it. Put the lid on and turn it clockwise for a proper sealing. Select "MANUAL" and set the cooking time to 25 minutes. Cook on HIGH pressure.

After the beeping sound, press the "KEEP WARM/CANCEL" button. Turn the pressure handle to "Venting" for a quick pressure release.

Let cool completely before storing.

Storing:

When cooled, divide between 4 airtight containers. Place in the fridge and consume within 3 days. Simply heat in the microwave. To freeze, transfer the chicken to 4 Ziploc bags and place in the freezer. Freeze for up to 3 months. Defrost in the fridge overnight and heat for a few minutes.

Nutrition facts per serving:

Calories Calories 240, Protein 25g, Total Carbs 4g, Net Carbs 2.5g, Total Fat 28g, Saturated Fat 11g, Fiber 1.5g, Sodium 250mg

Chicken Breast with Button Mushrooms and Coconut

Preparation time: 10 minutes | Cooking time: 15 minutes | Servings: 4

Ingredients:

4 Chicken Breasts, boneless and skinless
⅔ cup Chicken Broth
1 can Coconut Cream
1 pound White Button Mushrooms, sliced
2 tbsp Arrowroot
2 tbsp Water
Salt and Pepper, to taste
¼ tsp Garlic Powder

Instructions:

Combine the broth and coconut cream in your Instant Pot. Stir in the garlic powder and season with some salt and pepper. Season the breasts with salt and pepper as well, and then place them inside the Instant Pot. Stir in the mushrooms. Close the lid. Turn it clockwise for a proper sealing. After the chime, select "MANUAL" and set the cooking time to 10 minutes. Cook on HIGH pressure.

When the timer goes off, press the "KEEP WARM/CANCEL" button. Release the pressure quickly by moving the handle to "Venting". Open the lid carefully.

Transfer the chicken to a plate. Whisk the water and arrowroot together and stir the mixture into the sauce. Set the Instant Pot to "SAUTE" and cook for a couple of minutes, until thickened. Return the chicken to the pot and cook for another minute.

Let cool completely before storing.

Storing:

When cooled, divide between 4 airtight containers. Place in the fridge and consume within 3 days. Simply heat in the microwave. To freeze, transfer the chicken to 4 Ziploc bags and place in the freezer. Freeze for up to 3 months. Defrost in the fridge overnight and heat for a few minutes.

Nutrition facts per serving:

Calories 370, Protein 35g, Total Carbs 4g, Net Carbs 2g, Total Fat 29g, Saturated Fat 10g, Fiber 2g, Sodium 450mg

Tarragon and Mushroom Chicken

Preparation time: 10 minutes | Cooking time: 15 minutes | Servings: 4

Ingredients:

1 tbsp chopped Tarragon
4 Chicken Thighs
1 tbsp Tomato Paste
¼ cup Butter
2 cups sliced Mushrooms
1 ¼ cups Chicken Broth
Salt and Pepper, to taste
1 tsp minced Garlic

Instructions:

Set your Instant Pot to "SAUTE" and add the butter to it. When melted, add the garlic and cook for 30 seconds. Season the chicken thighs with some salt and pepper and place them inside the Instant Pot. Cook for about 3 minutes or so, or until golden on all sides. Transfer the chicken thighs to a plate.

Add the mushrooms and tomato paste to the pot and cook for about 2 minutes. Then, pour the broth into the Instant Pot and stir to combine the mixture. Stir in the tarragon and then return the chicken thighs to the pot. Put the lid on and turn it clockwise for a proper sealing. Select "MANUAL" and set the cooking time to 10 minutes. Cook on HIGH pressure.

After the beep, hit "KEEP WARM/CANCEL". Turn the pressure handle to "Venting" for a quick pressure release and open the lid carefully.

Let cool completely before storing.

Storing:

When cooled, divide between 4 airtight containers. Place in the fridge and consume within 3 days. Simply heat in the microwave. To freeze, transfer the chicken to 4 Ziploc bags and place in the freezer. Freeze for up to 3 months. Defrost in the fridge overnight and heat for a few minutes.

Nutrition facts per serving:

Calories 260, Protein 19g, Total Carbs 3.9g, Net Carbs 2.2g, Total Fat 24g, Saturated Fat 16g, Fiber 3,7g, Sodium 495mg

Simple Alfredo Shredded Chicken

Preparation time: 10 minutes | Cooking time: 25 minutes | Servings: 6

Ingredients:

1 ½ pound boneless and skinless Chicken Breast
½ cup Keto Alfredo Sauce
½ cup Heavy Cream
¼ cup Chicken Broth
¼ tsp Garlic Powder
Salt and Pepper, to taste

Instructions:

Whisk together the broth, heavy cream, and Alfredo sauce.

Season the chicken, as well as the sauce, with some salt and pepper, and sprinkle the garlic powder over.

Close the lid. To seal, turn the lid clockwise. You should hear a chime.

After the chime, hit "MANUAL" and set the cooking time to 25 minutes. Make sure to cook on HIGH pressure.

When the timer goes off, press the "KEEP WARM/CANCEL" button.

Move the pressure handle from "Sealing" to "Venting" for a quick pressure release and open the lid carefully.

Grab two forks and shred the chicken inside the Instant Pot. Stir to combine well.

Let cool completely before storing.

Storing:

When cooled, divide between 6 airtight containers. Place in the fridge and consume within 3 days. Simply heat in the microwave. To freeze, transfer the chicken to 4 Ziploc bags and place in the freezer. Freeze for up to 3 months. Defrost in the fridge overnight and heat for a few minutes.

Nutrition facts per serving:

Calories 280, Protein 24g, Total Carbs 4g, Net Carbs 3.2g, Total Fat 12g, Saturated Fat 5g, Fiber 1.8g, Sodium 610mg

Leftover Chicken in a Spicy Tomato Sauce

Preparation time: 10 minutes | Cooking time: 6 minutes | Servings: 4

Ingredients:

2 cups cooked and shredded Chicken Meat
14 ounces diced canned Tomatoes
¼ cup Chicken Broth
1 tsp Chili Powder
¼ tsp Garlic Powder
¼ tsp Pepper
¼ tsp Salt
1 cup Cauliflower Rice
¼ cup Sour Cream

Instructions:

Place all of the ingredients inside your Instant Pot.

Give the mixture a good stir so that everything is well combined and the chicken is fully coated with the sauce.

Put the lid on and turn it clockwise for a proper sealing. After you hear the chime, press the "MANUAL" button. Then, set the cooking time to 6 minutes. Cook on HIGH pressure.

Select the "KEEP WARM/CANCEL" button after the beeping sound.

Turn the pressure handle to "Venting" for a quick pressure release and open the lid carefully.

Let cool completely before storing.

Storing:

When cooled, divide between 4 airtight containers. Place in the fridge and consume within 3 days. Simply heat in the microwave. To freeze, divide among 4 Ziploc bags and place in the freezer in a single layer. When frozen, you can stack the bags on top of each other. Freeze for up to 3 months. Defrost in the fridge overnight and heat for a few minutes.

Nutrition facts per serving:

Calories 310, Protein 19g, Total Carbs 4g, Net Carbs 2.2g, Total Fat 18g, Saturated Fat 10g, Fiber 3.8g, Sodium 590mg

Turkey Stew with Veggies

Preparation time: 10 minutes | Cooking time: 15 minutes | Servings: 4

Ingredients:

2 Turkey Breasts, chopped finely
1 cup Broccoli Florets
1 cup chopped Celery
1 cup chopped Snow Peas
1 cup Spinach
1 cup diced Tomatoes
3 cups Chicken Broth
Salt and Pepper, to taste
2 tbsp Butter
Salt and Pepper, to taste

Instructions:

Set your Instant Pot to "SAUTE" and add the butter to it. Season the turkey with some salt and peppers and add the pieces to the pot. Cook for about 5 minutes, or until they are golden and cooked through. Stir in the tomatoes and celery and cook for another 2 minutes.

Stir in the remaining ingredients and season with some more salt and pepper. Put the lid on and turn it clockwise to seal. Select "MANUAL" and set the cooking time to 8 minutes. Cook on HIGH pressure.

When the timer goes off, press the "KEEP WARM/CANCEL" button.

Do a natural pressure release by allowing the pressure valve to drop on its own. Let cool completely before storing.

Storing:

When cooled, divide between 4 airtight containers. Place in the fridge and consume within 3 days. Simply heat in the microwave. To freeze, divide among 4 Ziploc bags and place in the freezer in a single layer. When frozen, you can stack the bags on top of each other. Freeze for up to 3 months. Defrost in the fridge overnight and heat for a few minutes.

Nutrition facts per serving:

Calories 310, Protein 22g, Total Carbs 4.3g, Net Carbs 3.9g, Total Fat 12g, Saturated Fat 5g, Fiber 4.1g, Sodium 555mg

Turkey Breast in Italian Sauce

Preparation time: 10 minutes | Cooking time: 20 minutes | Servings: 6

Ingredients:

1 cup Tomato Sauce

½ cup Sour Cream

1 tsp Italian Seasoning

⅓ cup chopped Sun-Dried Tomatoes

1 pound Turkey Breasts, chopped

1 tbsp Olive Oil

1 tbsp chopped Basil

2 Garlic Cloves, minced

2 tbsp grated Parmesan Cheese

Instructions:

Set your Instant Pot to "SAUTE" and add the olive oil to it. When hot and sizzling, add the garlic and cook for about 30-60 seconds. Then, add the turkey breasts, season with salt and pepper, and cooked until they become golden. Stir in the tomato sauce, sour cream, sun-dried tomatoes, and Italian seasoning.

Put the lid on and turn it clockwise to seal well. Select "MANUAL" and set the cooking time to 10 minutes. Cook on HIGH pressure.

When the timer goes off, press the "KEEP WARM/CANCEL" button. Turn the pressure handle to "Venting" for a quick pressure release and open the lid carefully. Stir in the basil and sprinkle with Parmesan cheese.

Let cool completely before storing.

Storing:

When cooled, divide between 6 airtight containers. Place in the fridge and consume within 3 days. Simply heat in the microwave. To freeze, transfer the chicken to 4 Ziploc bags and place in the freezer. Freeze for up to 3 months. Defrost in the fridge overnight and heat for a few minutes.

Nutrition facts per serving:

Calories 350, Protein 31g, Total Carbs 5g, Net Carbs 2.1g, Total Fat 22g, Saturated Fat 10g, Fiber 2.9g, Sodium 590mg

Mexican "Risotto" with Turkey

Preparation time: 10 minutes | Cooking time: 23 minutes | Servings: 4

Ingredients:

4 cups Cauliflower Rice
2 Turley Breasts
1 ½ cup Chicken Broth
¼ tsp Cumin
¼ tsp Garlic Powder
¼ Red Onion, diced
1 Jalapeno, diced and seeded
½ cup mild Salsa
½ cup Tomato Sauce
Salt and Pepper, to taste
1 tbsp Olive Oil

Instructions:

Pour the broth into the Instant Pot. Season the turkey with some salt and pepper and place it inside the Instant Pot. Put the lid on and turn it clockwise for a proper sealing. Select "MANUAL" and set the cooking time to 15 minutes. Cook on HIGH pressure.

After the beeping sound, press the "KEEP WARM/CANCEL" button. Move the pressure handle to "Venting" for a quick pressure release and open the lid carefully. Transfer the turkey to a cutting board. Grab two forks and shred the meat well.

Discard the broth from the Instant Pot and wipe the pot clean. Set it to "SAUTE: and add the olive oil to it. When hot, add the onions and cook until soft. Then, stir in the remaining ingredients, including the turkey, and cook for about 5 minutes on SAUTE.

Let cool completely before storing.

Storing:

When cooled, divide between 4 airtight containers. Place in the fridge and consume within 3 days. Simply heat in the microwave. To freeze, transfer the turkey to 4 Ziploc bags and place in the freezer. Freeze for up to 3 months. Defrost in the fridge overnight and heat for a few minutes.

Nutrition facts per serving:

Calories 350, Protein 18g, Total Carbs 5g, Net Carbs 2.5g, Total Fat 22g, Saturated Fat 10g, Fiber 2g, Sodium 495mg

Simple Worcestershire Turkey Cubes

Preparation time: 10 minutes | Cooking time: 14 minutes | Servings: 4

Ingredients:

1 pound Turkey Breast
1 ½ cups Chicken Broth
1 tbsp Worcestershire Sauce
1 cup Sour Cream
¼ cup grated Parmesan Cheese
1 tsp Dijon Mustard
¼ tsp Garlic Powder
Salt and Pepper, to taste

Instructions:

Place the turkey and broth inside the Instant Pot and close the lid.

Turn it clockwise to seal and then select the "MANUAL" cooking mode. Set the cooking time to 12 minutes. Cook on HIGH pressure.

When the timer goes off, press the "KEEP WARM/CANCEL" button.

Turn the pressure handle to "Venting" for a quick pressure release and open the lid carefully. Transfer the turkey to a cutting board and cut into cubes.

Discard the broth from the Instant Pot and wipe the pot clean. Whisk together the remaining ingredients and place the Turkey cubes inside. Cook on "SAUTE" for a minute or two.

Let cool completely before storing.

Storing:

When cooled, divide between 4 airtight containers. Place in the fridge and consume within 3 days. Simply heat in the microwave. To freeze, transfer the turkey to 4 Ziploc bags and place in the freezer. Freeze for up to 3 months. Defrost in the fridge overnight and heat for a few minutes.

Nutrition facts per serving:

Calories 280, Protein 27g, Total Carbs 4g, Net Carbs 2.5g, Total Fat 21g, Saturated Fat 14g, Fiber 1.5g, Sodium 710mg

Sweet and Chili Goose Breast

Preparation time: 10 minutes | Cooking time: 20 minutes | Servings: 6

Ingredients:

1 pound Goose Breasts
1 cup Chicken Broth
3 tbsp Tamari Sauce
1 tbsp Sweetener
3 tbsp Low-Carb Chili Sauce
Salt and Pepper, to taste

Instructions:

Season the goose breasts with some salt and pepper and place them inside the Instant Pot.

In a bowl, whisk together all of the remaining ingredients and pour the mixture over the goose.

Put the lid on and turn it clockwise for a proper sealing.

Select "MANUAL" and set the cooking time to 15 minutes. Cook on HIGH pressure.

After the alarm goes off, press the "KEEP WARM/CANCEL" button.

Turn the handle from "Sealing" to "Venting" for a quick pressure release and open the lid carefully.

Let cool completely before storing.

Storing:

When cooled, divide between 6 airtight containers. Place in the fridge and consume within 3 days. Simply heat in the microwave. To freeze, transfer the goose to 4 Ziploc bags and place in the freezer. Freeze for up to 3 months. Defrost in the fridge overnight and heat for a few minutes.

Nutrition facts per serving:

Calories 310, Protein 28g, Total Carbs 4g, Net Carbs 2.5g, Total Fat 19g, Saturated Fat 13g, Fiber 1.5g, Sodium 550mg

Creamy Duck with Spinach

Preparation time: 10 minutes | Cooking time: 13 minutes | Servings: 4

Ingredients:

1 pound Duck Breasts
2 cups Spinach
¼ cup grated Parmesan Cheese
1 cup Heavy Cream
8 ounces Cream Cheese
¼ cup Chicken Broth
1 tbsp Olive Oil
1 tsp minced Garlic
Salt and Pepper, to taste

Instructions:

Set your Instant Pot to "SAUTE" and add the olive oil to it. When hot, add the garlic and cook for a minute.

Add the duck and cook it for about 3-4 minutes per side, until golden.

Transfer to a plate and slice it thinly. Whisk together the remaining ingredients in the Instant Pot and place the duck inside.

Put the lid on and turn it clockwise for a proper sealing.

Select "MANUAL" and set the cooking time to 5 minutes. Cook on HIGH pressure.

When the timer goes off, press the "KEEP WARM/CANCEL" button.

Turn the pressure handle to "Venting" for a quick pressure release and open the lid carefully.

Let the duck cool completely before storing.

Storing:

When cooled, divide between 4 airtight containers. Place in the fridge and consume within 2-3 days. Simply heat in the microwave. To freeze, divide among 4 Ziploc bags and place in the freezer for up to 2-3 months. Defrost in the fridge overnight and heat for a few minutes.

Nutrition facts per serving:

Calories 355, Protein 30g, Total Carbs 4g, Net Carbs 2g, Total Fat 18g, Saturated Fat 9g, Fiber 2g, Sodium 420mg

RED MEAT RECIPES

Shredded Mexican Beef

Preparation time: 10 minutes | Cooking time: 13 minutes | Servings: 6

Ingredients:

2 pounds Chuck Roast
1 tsp Chili Powder
½ tsp Smoked Paprika
½ tsp Cumin
¼ cup Butter
1 ½ cups canned diced Tomatoes
1 cup Beef Broth
Salt and Pepper, to taste
½ tsp Garlic Powder

Instructions:

Set your Instant Pot to "SAUTE" and add the butter to it. When melted, add the beef and sear it well on all sides. Transfer the beef to a plate. Place the tomatoes and all of the spices in the pot and cook for about 2 minutes. Pour the broth over and stir to combine. Return the beef to the pot. Put the lid on and turn it clockwise to seal. When you hear the sealing chime, press "MANUAL" and set the cooking time to 20 minutes. Cook on HIGH pressure.

After the alarm goes off, press the "KEEP WARM/CANCEL" button. Move the pressure handle to "Venting" to release the pressure quickly and open the lid carefully. Grab two forks and shred the beef inside the pot. Stir to coat it well.

Let cool completely before storing.

Storing:

When cooled, divide between 6 airtight containers. Place in the fridge and consume within 3 days. To freeze, divide among 8 Ziploc bags and freeze. Consume within 3 months. Defrost in the fridge overnight and heat for a few minutes.

Nutrition facts per serving:

Calories 260, Protein 30g, Total Carbs 3g, Net Carbs 1g, Total Fat 20g, Saturated Fat 9g, Fiber 2g, Sodium 635mg

Tamari Steak with Tomatoes

Preparation time: 10 minutes | Cooking time: 15 minutes | Servings: 4

Ingredients:

2 tbsp low-carb Tamari
1 pound Beef Steak, sliced
2 Tomatoes, chopped
1 tsp Sweetener
1 tsp Vinegar
2 Garlic Cloves, minced
1 small Onion, diced
2 tbsp Olive Oil
½ cup Beef Broth
Salt and Pepper, to taste

Instructions:

Set your Instant Pot to "SAUTE" and add half of the oil to it. When hot, add the beef slices. Season them with some salt and pepper and cook until they are browned, for a few minutes. Transfer the beef to a plate and then add the rest of the oil to the Instant Pot. When the oil is hot, add the onions and cook for 2-3 minutes.

Then, stir in the garlic but do not cook more than a minute. Stir in the tomatoes and cook for another 2 minutes. Stir in the remaining ingredients and return the beef to the pot. Put the lid on and turn it clockwise for a proper sealing. Select "MANUAL" and set the cooking time to 5 minutes. Cook on HIGH pressure.

After the beep, press the "KEEP WARM/CANCEL" button. Turn the pressure handle to "Venting" for a quick pressure release and open the lid carefully.

Let cool completely before storing.

Storing:

When cooled, divide between 4 airtight containers (or one large if you are planning on heating the whole thing in a couple of days). Place in the fridge and consume within 3 days. To freeze, divide among 8 small Ziploc bags and place in the freezer. Freeze for up to 3 months. Defrost in the fridge overnight and heat for a few minutes.

Nutrition facts per serving:

Calories 300, Protein 28g, Total Carbs 5g, Net Carbs 2g, Total Fat 15g, Saturated Fat 8g, Fiber 1g, Sodium 480mg

Meatloaf with Cheddar

Preparation time: 10 minutes | Cooking time: 30 minutes | Servings: 8

Ingredients:

1 ½ cups Water
2 tbsp Almond Flour
2 pounds ground Beef
1 small Onion, grated
½ tsp minced Garlic
1 Egg
2 tbsp grated Parmesan Cheese
½ cup Cheddar Cubes
¼ tsp Smoked Paprika
¼ tsp Italian Seasoning
Salt and Pepper, to taste

Instructions:

Pour the water into the Instant Pot and lower the trivet. Grease a baking dish that fits inside the Instant Pot with some cooking spray, and set it aside.

Place all of the ingredients, except the cheddar cheese, in a large bowl. Mix with your hands until the mixture is well combined. When fully incorporated, place half of the meat mixture inside the greased baking dish. Flatten it out and then top it with the cheddar cubes.

Top with the rest of the beef mixture, flattening it to make an even layer. Place the dish on top of the trivet and close the lid. Seal by turning the lid clockwise.. Select "MANUAL" and set the cooking time to 30 minutes. Cook on HIGH pressure.

When the timer goes off, select "KEEP WARM/CANCEL". Move the handle to "Venting" for a quick pressure release and then open the lid carefully. Allow to cool completely.

Storing:

Divide the meatloaf slices between 8 airtight containers. Place in the fridge and consume within 3 days. Simply heat in the microwave. To freeze, divide among 4 Ziploc bags and place in the freezer. Consume within 3 months. Defrost in the fridge overnight and heat for a few minutes.

Nutrition facts per serving:

Calories 270, Protein 27g, Total Carbs 2g, Net Carbs 2g, Total Fat 17g, Saturated Fat 9.8g, Fiber 0g, Sodium 595mg

Beef and "Rice"

Preparation time: 10 minutes | Cooking time: 14 minutes | Servings: 4

Ingredients:

1 pound Ground Beef
½ cup Beef Broth
1 small Onion, diced
¼ tsp Garlic Powder
3 cups Cauliflower Rice
1 tbsp Butter
2 tbsp Tomato Paste
¼ tsp dried Parsley
Salt and Pepper, to taste

Instructions:

Set your Instant Pot to "SAUTE" and add the butter to it. When melted, add the diced onion and saute for 2-3 minutes. When the onions are soft stir in the beef. Season with some salt and pepper and then cook the beef for a few minutes, until it becomes brown. Stir in all of the remaining ingredients.

Put the lid on and turn it clockwise for a proper sealing. Press the "MANUAL" button and set the cooking time to 5 minutes. Make sure to cook on HIGH pressure.

When the timer goes off, hit the "KEEP WARM/CANCEL" button. Release the pressure quickly by moving the pressure handle from "Sealing" to Venting". Open the lid gently.

Let cool completely before storing.

Storing:

When cooled, divide between 4 airtight containers (or one large if you are planning on serving it all at once). Place in the fridge and consume within 3 days. To freeze, divide among 4 Ziploc bags and place in the freezer. Freeze for up to 3 months. Defrost in the fridge overnight and heat for a few minutes.

Nutrition facts per serving:

Calories 290, Protein 32g, Total Carbs 5g, Net Carbs 2g, Total Fat 18g, Saturated Fat 10g, Fiber 1g, Sodium 620mg

Swedish Meatballs

Preparation time: 10 | Cooking time: 18 minutes | Servings: 4

Ingredients:

1 pound Ground Beef
1 Egg
1 cup shredded Pepper Jack Cheese
¼ tsp Cumin
½ Onion, diced
¼ tsp Pepper
½ cup Heavy Cream
1 cup Beef Broth
2 tsp minced Garlic
2 tbsp Olive Oil
1 tsp low-carb Tamari
½ tsp Fish Sauce
1 tsp Mustard

Instructions:

In a bowl, place the first 6 ingredients. Mix the mixture with your hands until well combined and then shape it into meatballs. Set your Instant Pot to "SAUTE" and add half of the oil to it. When hot, add the meatballs and cook them until they become browned on all side. Transfer the meatballs to a plate.

Add the rest of the oil to the pot and then add the garlic. Cook for a minute or so, until really fragrant. Then, stir in the remaining ingredients. Drop the meatballs into the sauce, one by one, carefully. Put the lid on and turn it clockwise for a proper sealing. Choose the "MANUAL" cooking mode and set the cooking time to 10 minutes. Cook on HIGH pressure.

When the timer goes off, press the "KEEP WARM/CANCEL" button. Move the pressure handle to "Venting" to release the pressure quickly. Open the lid really carefully and allow to cool completely.

Storing:

When cooled, divide between 4 airtight containers. Place in the fridge and consume within 3 days. To freeze, divide among 4 Ziploc bags and place in the freezer. Freeze for up to 3 months. Defrost in the fridge overnight and heat for a few minutes.

Nutrition facts per serving:

Calories 310, Protein 28g, Total Carbs 4g, Net Carbs 3.2g, Total Fat 16g, Saturated Fat 9g, Fiber 0.8g, Sodium 710mg

Spicy Pulled Pork

Preparation time: 10 | Cooking time: 13 minutes | Servings: 4

Ingredients:

Ingredients:
2 pounds Pork Shoulder
1 tsp Chili Powder
½ tsp Smoked Paprika
½ tsp Cumin
½ tsp Onion Powder
½ tsp Garlic Salt
¼ tsp Pepper
1 ½ cups Beef Broth
1 tbsp Coconut Oil

Instructions:

Set your Instant Pot to "SAUTE" and add the oil to it. While the oil is melting, combine all of the spices in a bowl and massage the pork with the mixture. When the coconut oil is fully melted, add the pork to the Instant Pot.

Sear well on all sides, until browned. Pour the broth over and put the lid of the Instant Pot on. Seal by turning the pot clockwise. You should be able to hear a chime.

Select "MEAT/STEW" and set the cooking time to 35 minutes. Cook on HIGH pressure.

When the timer goes off, press the "KEEP WARM/CANCEL" button. Turn the pressure handle to "Venting" for a quick pressure release and open the lid carefully.

Transfer the pork to a cutting board. Grab two forks and shred the meat well. Open the lid and allow to cool completely before storing.

Storing:

When cooled, divide between 4 airtight containers. Place in the fridge and consume within 3 days. To freeze, divide among 4 Ziploc bags and place in the freezer. Consume within 3 months. Defrost in the fridge overnight and heat for a few minutes.

Nutrition facts per serving:

Calories 295, Protein 28g, Total Carbs 0g, Net Carbs 0g, Total Fat 21g, Saturated Fat 11g, Fiber 0g, Sodium 400mg

Creamy Pork with Bacon

Preparation time: 10 | Cooking time: 13 minutes | Servings: 4

Ingredients:

⅓ cup Heavy Cream
1 cup Chicken Broth
1 ½ tsp Arrowroot
1 tbsp Water
3 Bacon Slices, chopped
1 tsp Olive Oil
1 pound Pork Tenderloin, cut into strips
1 tsp dried Thyme
¼ tsp Garlic Powder
Salt and Pepper, to taste

Instructions:

Set your Instant Pot to "SAUTE" and add the bacon pieces to it. Cook for a few minutes, until crispy. Add the olive oil and heat it until sizzling.

Then, add the pork strips and season with some salt and pepper. Cook the pork until browned on all sides. Pour the broth over and stir in the spices. Put the lid on and turn it clockwise for a proper sealing. Select "MANUAL" and set the cooking time to 15 minutes. Cook on HIGH pressure.

After the beep, press the "KEEP WARM/CANCEL" button. Turn the pressure handle to "Venting" for a quick pressure release and open the lid carefully.

Stir in the heavy cream and cook on "SAUTE" for 2 minutes or so. Whisk together the arrowroot and water and stir the mixture into the sauce. Season with some extra salt and pepper. Let cool completely.

Storing:

When cooled, divide between airtight containers. Place in the fridge and consume within 3 days. To freeze, divide among 4 Ziploc bags and place in the freezer. Freeze for up to 3 months. Defrost in the fridge overnight and heat for a few minutes.

Nutrition facts per serving:

Calories 355, Protein 28g, Total Carbs 3g, Net Carbs 2g, Total Fat 25g, Saturated Fat 16g, Fiber 1g, Sodium 750mg

Lamb Kofta in Tomato Sauce

Preparation time: 10 minutes | Cooking time: 20 minutes | Servings: 4

Ingredients:

1 pound ground Lamb
¼ Onion, grated
2 tbsp grated Parmesan Cheese
2 tbsp Almond Flour
1 Egg
¼ tsp Cayenne Pepper
¼ tsp Garlic Powder
1 cup Tomato Sauce
½ cup chopped Tomatoes
1 tbsp Olive Oil
1 tbsp chopped Cilantro
Salt and Pepper, to taste

Instructions:

Place the first 6 ingredients in a large bowl. Mix with your hands until the mixture is well combined. Shape the mixture into 4 koftas. Set your Instant Pot to "SAUTE" and add the olive oil to it. Add the koftas and cook for about 2 minutes per side. Place the remaining ingredients in a bowl and stir to combine. POur the sauce over the koftas and close the lid. Turn it clockwise for a proper sealing. Select "MANUAL" and set the cooking time to 15 minutes. Cook on HIGH pressure.

When the timer goes off, press the "KEEP WARM/CANCEL" button. Turn the pressure handle to "Venting" for a quick pressure release and open the lid carefully. Allow to cool before storing.

Storing:

When cooled, place the lamb in airtight containers. Place in the fridge and consume within 3 days. To freeze, divide among 4 Ziploc bags and place in the freezer. Freeze for up to 3 months.

Defrost in the fridge overnight and heat for a few minutes.

Nutrition facts per serving:

Calories 410, Protein 31g, Total Carbs 5g, Net Carbs 4g, Total Fat 22g, Saturated Fat 11g, Fiber 1g, Sodium 515mg

Cinnamon and Cocoa Lamb Shoulder

Preparation time: 15 minutes | Cooking time: 35 minutes | Servings: 4

Ingredients:

1 pound Lamb Shoulder, boneless
1 tsp Cocoa Powder
¼ tsp Cinnamon Powder
½ tsp Sweetener
½ tsp Garlic Powder
½ tsp Onion Flakes
¼ tsp Cayenne Pepper
1 tbsp Olive Oil
Salt and Pepper, to taste
1 ½ cups Beef Broth

Instructions:

Instructions:

Set your Instant Pot to "SAUTE" and add the olive oil. While heating, combine all of the spices in a bowl. Rub the spice mixture into the lamb and place it in the Instant Pot. Sear on all sides for about 5 minutes in total.

Pour the broth around the lamb and close the lid. To seal, just turn the lid clockwise.

When you hear the chiming sound, select "MANUAL". Set the cooking time to 30 minutes. Cook on HIGH pressure.

When the timer goes off, press the "KEEP WARM/CANCEL" button. Turn the pressure handle to "Venting" for a quick pressure release and open the lid carefully.

Let cool completely before storing.

Storing:

When cooled, divide between 4 airtight containers. Place in the fridge and consume within 3 days. To freeze, divide among 4 Ziploc bags and place in the freezer. Consume within months. Defrost in the fridge overnight and heat for a few minutes.

Nutrition facts per serving:

Calories 290, Protein 27g, Total Carbs 0g, Net Carbs 0g, Total Fat 25g, Saturated Fat 12g, Fiber 0g, Sodium 375mg

Mutton Curry

Preparation time: 10 minutes | Cooking time: 33 minutes | Servings: 4

Ingredients:

1 pound Mutton, chopped
1 tsp Curry Powder
1 tsp minced Ginger
2 tsp minced Garlic
¼ tsp Cinnamon Powder
1 Bay Leaf
1 tsp Coriander Powder
1 Onion, diced
14 ounces canned diced Tomatoes
2 cups Beef Broth
1 tbsp Olive Oil

Instructions:

Set your Instant Pot to "SAUTE" and add the olive oil to it. When hot, add the onions and garlic and cook for 2 minutes.

Add the mutton pieces and cook for a few more minutes, until browned on all sides. Stir in the spices and cook for 30 seconds more. Add the rest of the ingredients, stir to combine well, and then close the lid.

Turn the lid clockwise for a proper sealing. Select "MEAT/STEW" and set the cooking time to 25 minutes. Cook on HIGH pressure.

After the beep, select the "KEEP WARM/CANCEL" button. Move the pressure handle to "Venting" for a quick pressure release and open the lid carefully Let the meat cool down completely before storing.

Storing:

When cooled, divide between 4 airtight containers. Place in the fridge and consume within 3 days. To freeze, divide among 6 Ziploc bags and place in the freezer. Consume within 3 months. Defrost in the fridge overnight and heat for a few minutes.

Nutrition facts per serving:

Calories 380, Protein 30g, Total Carbs 5g, Net Carbs 2.8g, Total Fat 23g, Saturated Fat 16g, Fiber 1.2g, Sodium 355mg

FISH AND SEAFOOD RECIPES

Stewed Shellfish

Preparation time: 15 minutes | Cooking time: 11 minutes | Servings: 4

Ingredients:

1 cup Scallops
2 cups Mussels
1 Onion, diced
1 tbsp Butter or Coconut Oil
2 Bell Peppers, diced
2 cups Cauliflower Rice
2 cups Fish Stock
Pinch of Saffron
Salt and Pepper, to taste

Instructions:

Set your Instant Pot to "SAUTE" and add the coconut oil or butter to it. When melted, add the onions and bell peppers and cook for about 3 minutes.

When the veggies become softened, stir in the saffron and scallops and cook for additional 2 minutes.

Add the rest of the ingredients to the pot. Give the mixture a good stir to combine. Put the lid on and turn it clockwise to seal.

Select the "MANUAL" cooking mode and then set the cooking time to 6 minutes. Cook on HIGH pressure.

After the beep, select the "KEEP WARM/CANCEL" button. Allow the pressure valve to drop on its own for a natural pressure release. Let cool completely.

Storing:

Divide between 4 airtight containers and put in the fridge. You can consume for up to 3 days. To freeze, divide between 4 Ziploc bags or airtight containers and place in the freezer for up to 3 months. Defrost in the fridge and microwave for a few minutes before serving.

Nutrition facts per serving:

Calories 195, Protein 20g, Total Carbs 5g, Net Carbs 2.6g, Total Fat 7g, Saturated Fat 2.2g, Fiber 3.4g, Sodium 510mg

Cheesy Tilapia

Preparation time: 10 minutes | Cooking time: 10 minutes | Servings: 4

Ingredients:

1 tbsp Butter
12 ounces Tilapia Fillets
¼ Onion, diced
½ cup Heavy Cream

¼ tsp Garlic Powder
5 ounces shredded Cheddar Cheese
Salt and Pepper, to taste

Instructions:

Set your Instant Pot to "SAUTE" and add the butter to it. When melted, add the onions and cook for about 3 minutes. When the onions become softened, add the tilapia and season with some salt and pepper. Cook for about 2 minutes on both sides, or until slightly golden. Pour the heavy cream over, sprinkle with the garlic powder and top with the cheese. Put the lid on and turn it clockwise to seal. Select "MANUAL" and set the cooking time to 5 minutes. Cook on HIGH pressure.

After the beep, select the "KEEP WARM/CANCEL" button. Turn the handle from "Sealing" to "Venting" for a quick pressure release and open the lid carefully.

Storing:

Divide the salad between 4 airtight containers and put in the fridge. You can use them for up to 3 days. To freeze, divide between 6 Ziploc bags or airtight containers and place in the freezer for up to 3 months. Defrost in the fridge and enjoy cold.

Nutrition facts per serving:

Calories 195, Protein 18g, Total Carbs 4.5g, Net Carbs 2.5g, Total Fat 18g, Saturated Fat 10g, Fiber 1g, Sodium 320mg

Hot Anchovies

Preparation time: 10 minutes | Cooking time: 10 minutes | Servings: 4

Ingredients:

1 Chili, sliced
1 tsp Chili Powder
½ tsp Red Chili Flakes
10 ounces Anchovy

4 tbsp Butter
⅓ cup ground Almonds
1 tsp Dill
Salt and Pepper, to taste

Instructions:

Set your Instant Pot to "SAUTE" and add the butter to it. While the butter is melting and the Instant Pot is getting heated, combine the chili and all of the spices in a bowl. Cot the anchovy with the mixture well. When the butter is melted, add the anchovy to the Instant Pot and cook until browned, or about 4-5 minutes per side. Let cool completely.

Storing:

Divide between 4 airtight containers and put in the fridge. You can use them for up to 3 days. To freeze, divide between 4 Ziploc bags or airtight containers and place in the freezer for up to 3 months. Defrost in the fridge and microwave for a few minutes before serving.

Nutrition facts per serving:

Calories 350, Protein 28g, Total Carbs 3.5g, Net Carbs 3g, Total Fat 25g, Saturated Fat 12g, Fiber 0.5g, Sodium 455mg

Gingery and Orange Mackerel

Preparation time: 10 minutes | Cooking time: 6 minutes | Servings: 4

Ingredients:

3 Spring Onions, chopped
4 Mackerel Fillets
1 cup White Wine
1 1-inch piece of Ginger, thinly sliced

Juice and Zest of 1 Orange
1 tbsp Olive Oil
Salt and Pepper, to taste

Instructions:

Pour the wine and juice into your Instant Pot and stir in the zest, ginger, and spring onions. Brush the fish fillets with olive oil and sprinkle them with some salt and pepper. Place the mackerel in the steamer basket and lower the basket into the pot.

Close the lid of the Instant Pot and turn it clockwise to seal. Select "MANUAL" and set the cooking time to 6 minutes. Cook on HIGH pressure.

After you hear the beep, select the "KEEP WARM/CANCEL" button. Turn the pressure handle to "Venting" to do a quick pressure release and open the lid carefully.

Storing:

Divide between 4 airtight containers and put in the fridge. You can use them for up to 3 days. To freeze, divide between 4 Ziploc bags or airtight containers and place in the freezer for up to 3 months. Defrost in the fridge and microwave for a few minutes before serving.

Nutrition facts per serving:

Calories 240, Protein 35g, Total Carbs 4.5g, Net Carbs 2.3g, Total Fat 5g, Saturated Fat 1g, Fiber 1g, Sodium 380mg

VEGETABLES AND SIDE DISHES

Broccoli with Tomatoes

Preparation time: 10 minutes | Cooking time: 13 minutes | Servings: 4

Ingredients:

1 Broccoli Head, broken into florets
2 14-ounce cans diced Tomatoes
½ Onion, diced
1 tsp Garlic Powder
½ tsp Celery Seeds
1 tbsp Olive Oil
Salt and Pepper, to taste

Instructions:

Set your Instant Pot to "SAUTE" and add the olive oil to it. When hot and sizzling, add the onions and cook for 3 minutes.

Stir in the tomatoes and spices and cook for additional 2 minutes.

Add the broccoli florerts, stir to combine, and put the lid on. Seal the Instant Pot by turning the lid clockwise.

Select "MANUAL" and set the cooking time to 8 minutes. Cook on HIGH pressure.

When the alarm goes off, hit "KEEP WARM/CANCEL".

Move the pressure handle to "Venting" for a quick pressure release and then open the lid carefully.

Let cool completely.

Storing:

When cooled, divide between 4 airtight containers. Place in the fridge and consume within 3-4 days. To freeze, divide among 4 Ziploc bags and place in the freezer. Consume within 3 months. Defrost in the fridge overnight and heat for a few minutes.

Nutrition facts per serving:

Calories 150, Protein 9g, Total Carbs 5.6g, Net Carbs 2.7g, Total Fat 12g, Saturated Fat 4g, Fiber 2g, Sodium 180mg

Soft Cabbage with Garlic and Lemon

Preparation time: 10 minutes | Cooking time: 7 minutes | Servings: 4

Ingredients:

2 tsp minced Garlic
¼ cup Lemon Juice
1 tbsp Olive Oil
2 cups chopped Cabbage
1 cup Chicken or Vegie Broth
¼ tsp Onion Powder
Salt and Pepper, to taste

Instructions:

Combine the broth and cabbage to your instant pot. Put the lid on and turn it clockwise to seal well.

Then select "MANUAL" and set the cooking time to 5 minutes. Cook on HIGH pressure.

When the timer goes off, select the "KEEP WARM/CANCEL" button.

Do a quick pressure release by moving the handle from "Sealing" to "Venting".

Open the lid gently and transfer the cabbage to a plate. Discard the broth and wipe the pot clean.

Set the Instant Pot to "SAUTE" and add the olive oi to it. When hot, add the garlic and cook for 1 minute.

Stir in the cabbage and all of the seasoning. Stir in the lemon juice before serving. Allow to cool completely before storing.

Storing:

When cooled, divide between 3 airtight containers. Place in the fridge and consume within 3-4 days. To freeze, divide among 3 Ziploc bags and place in the freezer. Consume within 3 months. Defrost in the microwave and heat for a couple of minutes to enjoy warm.

Nutrition facts per serving:

Calories 80, Protein 3g, Total Carbs 3g, Net Carbs 2g, Total Fat 7g, Saturated Fat 3g, Fiber 1g, Sodium 70mg

Cheesy Green Beans

Preparation time: 15 minutes | Cooking time: 7 minutes | Servings: 4

Ingredients:

12 ounces Green Beans
2 cups Water
⅔ cup grated Parmesan Cheese
1 Egg
¼ tsp Garlic Powder
2 tbsp Olive Oil
¼ tsp Onion Powder
Salt and Pepper, to taste

Instructions:

Pour the water into the Instant Pot. Place the green beans inside the steamer basket and lower the basket into the water. Close the lid and set the Instant Pot to "MANUAL". With the "+" and "-" buttons, set the cooking time to 3 minutes. Cook on HIGH pressure.

When the timer goes off, select the "KEEP WARM/CANCEL" button. Turn the pressure handle to "Venting" to release the pressure quickly and open the lid carefully.

Remove the steamer basket using mittens. Discard the water and wipe the Instant Pot clean. Prepare an ice bath and place the green beans in it in order to speed up the cooling process.

Meanwhile, beat the egg and heat half of the olive oil in the Instant Pot on "SAUTE". Place all of the remaining ingredients in a bowl and stir to combine. Dip half of the green beans in egg first, then coat with the parmesan mixture. Place in the Instant Pot and cook for about a minute per side. Repeat with the remaining oil and green beans.

Let cool completely before storing.

Storing:

When cooled, divide between 4 airtight containers. Place in the fridge and consume within 3 days. To freeze transfer to a container and place in the freezer until just set. Divide between 4 Ziploc bags and arrange them in a single layer until frozen. Consume within 3 months. Defrost in the microwave and heat for a few minutes to enjoy warm.

Nutrition facts per serving:

Calories 110, Protein 9g, Total Carbs 5.9g, Net Carbs 2.3g, Total Fat 8g, Saturated Fat 2g, Fiber 6g, Sodium 150mg

Caramelized Peppers and Onions

Preparation time: 10 minutes | Cooking time: 10 minutes | Servings: 4

Ingredients:

2 Bell Peppers
1 ½ Red Onions
1 tbsp Olive Oil
1 tsp Basil
1 Garlic Clove, minced
1 tbsp Butter
Salt and Pepper, to taste
1 ½ cups Water

Instructions:

You can ski this step and go straight to caramelizing the veggies on SAUTE option, but this results in softer and more delicious side dish. Pour the water into the Instant Pot and lower the trivet.

Place the pepper and onions in a baking dish and place on top of the trivet. Close and seal the lid and hit "MANUAL". Set the cooking time to 5 minutes. Cook on HIGH pressure.

When the timer goes off, select the "KEEP WARM/CANCEL" button. Turn the pressure handle to "Venting" for a quick pressure release and open the lid carefully.

Transfer the veggies to a cutting board and chop them up. Meanwhile, heat the olive oil along with the butter in the Instant Pot on "SAUTE". When the butter is melted, add the garlic and cook for a minute.

Then, stir in the chopped veggies and all of the remaining ingredients and cook for 4 minutes.

Allow to cool completely before storing.

Storing:

When cooled, divide between 4 airtight containers. Place in the fridge and consume within 3-4 days. To freeze, divide among 4 Ziploc bags and place in the freezer. Consume within 3 months. Defrost in the fridge overnight or in the microwave, and heat for a few minutes.

Nutrition facts per serving:

Calories 95, Protein 2g, Total Carbs 3.5g, Net Carbs 2.4g, Total Fat 7g, Saturated Fat 3g, Fiber 2.5g, Sodium 120mg

Chili Green Beans with Coconut

Preparation time: 10 minutes | Cooking time: 10 minutes | Servings: 4

Ingredients:

¾ pound Green Beans, sliced crosswise

¾ cup shredded unsweetened Coconut

2 Chilies, seeded and diced

2 tsp minced Garlic

2 tbsp Butter

¼ tsp Cumin

½ tsp minced Ginger

½ cup Chicken Broth

Salt and Pepper, to taste

Instructions:

Set your Instant Pot to "SAUTE" and add the butter to it. When melted, add the ginger, chilies, and garlic, and cook for about a minute.

Then, stir in the green beans and cumin and cook for 2 minutes. Add the broth and coconut and give the mixture a good stir.

Put the lid on and turn it clockwise to seal. Choose the "MANUAL" cooking mode and set the cooking time to 3 minutes. Cook on HIGH pressure.

When the timer goes off, select the "KEEP WARM/CANCEL" Turn the pressure handle to "Venting" to do a quick pressure release and open the lid carefully. If there you want the beans 'drier', set the Instant Pot to "SAUTE" and cook for a few minutes until the liquid evaporates.

Allow to cool completely before storing.

Storing:

Divide between 4 airtight containers. Place in the fridge and consume within 3 days. To freeze, divide among 4 Ziploc bags and place in the freezer. Consume within 3 months. Defrost in the fridge overnight or in the microwave and heat to enjoy warm.

Nutrition facts per serving:

Calories 150, Protein 3g, Total Carbs 3.4g, Net Carbs 2g, Total Fat 15g, Saturated Fat 4.5g, Fiber 4g, Sodium 150mg

Soft and Cheesy Keto "Bread"

Preparation time: 10 minutes | Cooking time: 17 minutes | Servings: 4

Ingredients:

¾ cup Coconut Flour
8 ounces shredded Mozzarella Cheese
Pinch of Cumin
Pinch of Garlic Salt
Pinch of Pepper
1 ½ cups Water

Instructions:

Pour the water into the Instant Pot and lower the trivet. Arrange a baking dish with parchment paper and set it aside.

Place all of the remaining ingredients in a microwave-safe bowl stir to combine, and microwave for a few minutes, until the cheese is fully melted.

Stir the mixture once again and transfer to a lightly-floured working surface. With a rolling pin, roll out the dough, making a rectangle. Cut that rectangle into 4 triangles.

Arrange the triangles on the baking shit.

Place the baking shit on top of the trivet and put the lid on. Turn it clockwise to seal.

Select "MANUAL" and set the cooking time to 15 minutes. Cook on HIGH pressure.

When you hear the beep, select the "KEEP WARM/CANCEL" button.

Move the handle to "Venting" for a quick pressure release and open the lid carefully. Let cool completely.

Storing:

Divide between 4 airtight containers. Place in the fridge and consume within 3-4 days. To freeze, divide among 4 Ziploc bags and place in the freezer. Consume within 3 months. Defrost in the fridge overnight and enjoy warm.

Nutrition facts per serving:

Calories 230, Protein 17g, Total Carbs 7.5g, Net Carbs 2.2g, Total Fat 12g, Saturated Fat 2.5g, Fiber 8g, Sodium 150mg

Curried Eggplant

Preparation time: 10 minutes | Cooking time: 15 minutes | Servings: 4

Ingredients:

12 ounces Eggplants, sliced
1 tsp minced Garlic
1 tsp minced Ginger
1 Onion, diced
1 tsp Curry Powder
½ cup Tomato Sauce
⅔ cup Chicken Broth
2 tbsp Butter

Instructions:

Set your Instant Pot to "SAUTE" and add half of the butter to it. When melted, add the eggplants and cook until browned on both sides. Transfer them to a plate.

Add the remaining butter to the pan and cook until melted.

Add the onions and cook for 3 minutes. Stir in the garlic and ginger and cook for another minute. Stir in the remaining ingredients and return the eggplant slices to the Instant Pot.

Put the lid on and turn it clockwise to seal. Select "MANUAL" and set the cooking time to 7 minutes. Cook on HIGH pressure.

When the timer goes off, select the "KEEP WARM/CANCEL" button.

Do a quick pressure release by turning the handle to a "Venting" position. Let cool before storing.

Storing:

Divide between 4 airtight containers. Place in the fridge and consume within 3 days. To freeze, transfer in freezer molds or ice cube tray. Consume within 1-2 months.

Nutrition facts per serving:

Calories 145, Protein 2g, Total Carbs 4.8g, Net Carbs 2.4g, Total Fat 14g, Saturated Fat 4.5g, Fiber 4g, Sodium 250mg

Creamy Spinach

Preparation time: 10 minutes | Cooking time: 5 minutes | Servings: 4

Ingredients:

1 pound Baby Spinach
¾ cup Heavy Cream
1 Tomato, diced
1 tsp Onion Powder
2 Garlic Cloves, minced
1 tbsp Butter
¼ cup Water
Salt and Pepper, to taste

Instructions:

Set your Instant Pot to "SAUTE" and add the butter to it.

When the butter is melted, add the garlic and cook for a minute. Stir in the tomato and cook for 2 more minutes.

Add the remaining ingredients and give the mixture a good stir to combine.

Put the lid on and turn it clockwise to seal.

Select "MANUAL" and set the cooking time to 2 minutes. Cook on HIGH pressure.

After the beep, press "KEEP WARM/CANCEL".

Turn the pressure handle from "Sealing" to "Venting" for a quick pressure release and open the lid carefully and let cool completely.

Storing:

Divide the spinach between 4 airtight containers. Place in the fridge and consume within 3 days. To freeze, divide among 4 Ziploc bags and place in the freezer. Consume within 3 months. Thaw in the fridge overnight or defrost in the microwave and heat in the microwave for a few minutes.

Nutrition facts per serving:

Calories 95, Protein 5g, Total Carbs 3g, Net Carbs 1g, Total Fat 8g, Saturated Fat 1g, Fiber 2g, Sodium 285mg

Soft Cumin Cabbage

Preparation time: 10 minutes | Cooking time: 8 minutes | Servings: 4

Ingredients:

1 ½ pounds Cabbage, cut into wedges

¼ cup Chicken Broth

3 tbsp Butter

½ tbsp Cumin

Salt and Pepper, to taste

Instructions:

Set your Instant Pot to "SAUTE" and add the butter to it. When melted, add the cabbage. Season with cumin, salt, and pepper, and cook for 3 minutes. Pour the broth over and stir to combine. Cook until the broth is reduced by half. Make sure to stir the cabbage well before serving. Of needed, season with some more salt and pepper, to taste. Open the lid and let the mixture cool completely before storing.

Storing:

When cooled, divide between 4 airtight containers. Place in the fridge and consume within 3 days. To freeze, divide among 4 Ziploc bags and place in the freezer. Consume within 3 months. Defrost in the fridge overnight or in the microwave and heat for a few minutes.

Nutrition facts per serving:

Calories 120, Protein 2.6g, Total Carbs 5.5g, Net Carbs 2.5g, Total Fat 9g, Saturated Fat 4g, Fiber 4g, Sodium 320mg

Kale "Pita Bread"

Preparation time: 15 minutes | Cooking time: 10 minutes | Servings: 4

Ingredients:

1 cup chopped Kale

½ cup Almond Flour

3 tbsp Butter

1 ½ tbsp Ground Flaxseed

¼ tsp Baking Powder

Pinch of Salt

Pinch of Cumin

2 tbsp grated Parmesan Cheese

1 ¼ cups Hot Water

Instructions:

Place the flour, flaxseed, cumin, salt, baking powder, and Parmesan, in a bowl and mix to combine. Pour the water gently while mixing, until a ball of dough is formed. Stir in the kale and knead the dough within the bowl.

Lightly flour your working surface and transfer the dough there. Divide the dough in 4 equal pieces and roll out each of them into a circle. Set your Instant Pot to "SAUTE" and add ¼ of the butter to it. When melted, add one "bread" and cook until it becomes slightly browned on both sides. Repeat with the remaining breads and butter. Allow the kale to cool completely before storing them.

Storing:

Divide the kale between 4 airtight containers. Place in the fridge and consume within 3-4 days. To freeze, divide among 4 Ziploc bags and place in the freezer. Consume within 3 months. Thaw in the fridge overnight and heat in the microwave for a few minutes.

Nutrition facts per serving:

Calories 240, Protein 8g, Total Carbs 8.1g, Net Carbs 3g, Total Fat 18g, Saturated Fat 4g, Fiber 19g, Sodium 195mg

Cheesy Cauliflower

Preparation time: 5 minutes | Cooking time: 7 minutes | Servings: 4

Ingredients:

1 Cauliflower Head, broken into florets
½ cup shredded Mozzarella Cheese
2 tbsp grated Parmesan Cheese

¼ cup Heavy Cream
Salt and Pepper, to taste
1 ½ cups Water

Instructions:

Pour the water into the Instant Pot and lower the trivet. Place the cauliflower florets in a baking dish and pour the heavy cream over. Season with some salt and pepper and stir to combine. Top the cauliflower with the cheeses. Place the baking dish on top of the trivet and close the lid. Put the lid on and turn it clockwise to seal. Select "MANUAL" and set the cooking time to 7 minutes. Cook on HIGH pressure.

When the timer goes off, select the "KEEP WARM/CANCEL" button. Turn the pressure handle to "Venting" for a quick pressure release and open the lid carefully. Let cool before storing.

Storing:

Store in the fridge in airtight containers. Best if consumed within 3 days. To freeze, divide among 4 Ziploc bags and place in the freezer. Consume within 3 months. Thaw in the fridge overnight and heat in the microwave for a few minutes.

Nutrition facts per serving:

Calories 180, Protein 5g, Total Carbs 3g, Net Carbs 2g, Total Fat 8g, Saturated Fat 2.2g, Fiber 1g, Sodium 150mg

Tofu & Tomatoes

Preparation time: 10 minutes | Cooking time: 9 minutes | Servings: 4

Ingredients:

14 ounces Tofu, cubed
2 tsp minced Garlic
14 ounces canned diced Tomatoes
¼ cup Chicken Broth
1 tbsp Olive Oil
1 Celery Stalk, diced
½ Onion, diced

Instructions:

Set your Instant Pot to "SAUTE" and add the olive oil to it.

When hot and sizzling, add the onions and celery and cook for about 3 minutes. Stir in the garlic and saute for a minute.

When the mixture becomes fragrant, stir in the tomatoes and tofu and cook for additional 2 minutes. Stir in the broth and put the lid on.

To seal the Instant Pot, just turn the lid clockwise.

When you hear the chime, you can press the "MANUAL" button. Using the "+" and "-" buttons, set the cooking time to 3 minutes. Cook on HIGH pressure.

When the timer goes off, select the "KEEP WARM/CANCEL" button.

Turn the pressure handle to "Venting" to release the pressure quickly.

Open the lid carefully. Let cool completely.

Storing:

Divide the tofu between 4 airtight containers. Place in the fridge and consume within 3-4 days. To freeze, divide among 2 Ziploc bags and place in the freezer. Consume within 3 months. Defrost in the microwave and heat in the microwave for a few minutes.

Nutrition facts per serving:

Calories 220, Protein 13g, Total Carbs 8g, Net Carbs 3g, Total Fat 18g, Saturated Fat 5.9g, Fiber 2g, Sodium 410mg

Tomato & Celery Okra

Preparation time: 10 minutes | Cooking time: 10 minutes | Servings: 4

Ingredients:

1 pound Okra
14 ounces canned diced Tomatoes
2 Celery Stalks, diced
½ tsp Italian Seasoning
½ small Onion, diced
½ tsp Garlic Powder
1 tbsp Butter
1 ½ cups Water

Instructions:

Pour the water inside the Instant Pot. Place the okra inside the steamer basket and then lower the basket into the pot.

Close the lid and seal by turning it clockwise. After you hear the chime, hit the "STEAM" button and set the cooking time to 4 minutes. Cook on HIGH pressure.

After the beep, select the "KEEP WARM/CANCEL" button. Do a quick pressure release by moving the pressure handle to a "Venting" position.

Open the lid carefully and transfer the okra to a cutting board. Slice thinly.

Discard the water from the Instant Pot and wipe the pot clean. Set the Instant Pot to "SAUTE" and add the butter to it.

When melted, add the onions and celery and cook for 3 minutes. Stir in the tomatoes and all spices and cook for 2 minutes. Stir in the okra and cook for 2 more minutes. Then let cool.

Storing:

Store in airtight containers. Place in the fridge and consume within 3 days. To freeze, divide among Ziploc bags and place in the freezer. Consume within 3 months. Defrost in the microwave and heat in the microwave for a few minutes.

Nutrition facts per serving:

Calories 95, Protein 5g, Total Carbs 6.8g, Net Carbs 3.6g, Total Fat 5g, Saturated Fat 0.5g, Fiber 2g, Sodium 245mg

Tofu and Bok Choy Bowl

Preparation time: 40 minutes | Cooking time: 20 minutes | Servings: 4

Ingredients:

1 Green Onion, diced
9 ounces Bok Choy, chopped
3 tbsp Olive Oil
2 tbsp Tamari
1 tsp Sweetener
Juice of ½ Lime
1 tbsp chopped Parsley

Tofu:

2 tsp minced Garlic
15 ounces Tofu, cubed
1 tbsp Tamari
1 tbsp Water
1 tbsp Sesame Oil
1 tbsp Vinegar
1 ½ cups Water

Instructions:

Pour the water into the Instant Pot and lower the trivet. Place all of the remaining tofu ingredients in a Ziploc bag.

Shake well to incorporate everything, and let the mixture sit for about 30 minutes to marinate. After 30 minutes, grease a baking dish with some cooking spray and arrange the tofu on it, evenly.

Place the dish on top of the trivet and put the lid of the Instant Pot on. Turn the lid clockwise to seal. Select the "MANUAL" cooking mode and set the cooking time to 20 minutes. Cook on HIGH pressure.

After you hear the beep, press the "KEEP WARM/CANCEL" button. Turn the pressure handle from "Sealing" to "Venting" for a quick pressure release and open the lid carefully.

Remove the dish with the tofu from the Instant Pot and let it sit for 2 minutes to cool a bit. Meanwhile, combine all of the remaining ingredients in a bowl. Stir in the tofu.

Let cool before storing.

Storing:

Divide between 4 airtight containers. Place in the fridge and consume within 3 days. To freeze, divide among 4 Ziploc bags and place in the freezer. Consume within 3 months. Thaw in the fridge overnight and heat in the microwave for a few minutes.

Nutrition facts per serving:

Calories 100, Protein 1g, Total Carbs 2g, Net Carbs 1g, Total Fat 14g, Saturated Fat 2g, Fiber 1g, Sodium 210mg

Chili and Zesty Brussel Sprouts

Preparation time: 10 minutes | Cooking time: 6 minutes | Servings: 4

Ingredients:

4 cups Brussel Sprouts
1 ½ cups Water
¼ tsp Salt
¼ tsp Pepper
½ Lemon Juice

¼ tsp Lemon Zest
1 Jalapeno, seeded and sliced
2 tbsp grated Parmesan Cheese
2 tbsp Olive Oil

Instructions:

Pour the water into the Instant Pot. Place the Brussel sprouts inside your steamer basket and then lower the basket into the water in the Instant Pot. Close the lid. To seal the Instant Pot, just turn the lid clockwise. After the chime, select "MANUAL" and set the cooking time to 6 minutes. Cook on HIGH pressure.

When the timer goes off, select the "KEEP WARM/CANCEL" button. Turn the pressure handle to "Venting" for a quick pressure release and open the lid carefully.

Transfer the Brussel sprouts to a bowl. In another bowl, whisk together the remaining ingredients. Pour over the sprouts and toss well to coat. Allow to cool before storing.

Storing:

Divide between 4 airtight containers. Place in the fridge and consume within 3 days. To freeze, divide among 4 Ziploc bags and place in the freezer. Consume within 3 months. Thaw in the fridge overnight and heat in the microwave for a few minutes.

Nutrition facts per serving:

Calories 180, Protein 4g, Total Carbs 4.6g, Net Carbs 3.2g, Total Fat 12g, Saturated Fat 3.5g, Fiber 1.8g, Sodium 315mg

Broccoli "Slaw"

Preparation time: 10 minutes | Cooking time: 4 minutes | Servings: 4

Ingredients:

4 Broccoli Stalks
1 ½ cups Water
1 tsp Celery Seeds
1 ½ tbsp Apple Cider Vinegar
⅓ cup Mayo
1 tbsp Sweetener
½ tbsp Dijon Mustard
Salt and Pepper, to taste

Instructions:

Pour the water into the Instant Pot and place the broccoli stalks inside the steamer basket.

Lower the basket into the water and then close the lid of the Instant Pot.

To seal the Instant Pot, turn the lid clockwise. Select "MANUAL" and set the cooking time to 4 minutes. Cook on HIGH pressure.

When the timer goes off, select the "KEEP WARM/CANCEL" button.

Turn the handle from "Sealing" to "Venting" for a quick pressure release and open the lid carefully.

Transfer the broccoli stalks to a cutting board and slice them thinly. Transfer to a bowl.

In another bowl, whisk together the remaining ingredients.

Pour the mayo mixture over the broccoli and toss well to coat.

Storing:

Divide the broccoli between 4 airtight containers. Place in the fridge and consume within 3 days. To freeze, divide among 4 Ziploc bags and place in the freezer. Consume within 3 months. Thaw in the fridge overnight and heat in the microwave for a few minutes.

Nutrition facts per serving:

Calories 120, Protein 6g, Total Carbs 5g, Net Carbs 3.5g, Total Fat 16g, Saturated Fat 7g, Fiber 1.5g, Sodium 360mg

Herbed Portobellos

Preparation time: 10 minutes | Cooking time: 23 minutes | Servings: 4

Ingredients:

12 ounces Portobello Mushrooms, sliced
2 tbsp Olive Oil
1 tbsp chopped Basil
1 Garlic Clove, minced
2 tbsp Balsamic Vinegar
1 tsp dried Thyme
1 tbsp chopped Cilantro
1 tsp dried Rosemary
½ small Onion, diced

Instructions:

You will not be cooking under pressure so you do not need any liquid for this recipe.

Set your Instant Pot to "SAUTE" and add the olive oil to it.

Add the onions and cook them for about 3 minutes. Add garlic and cook for 1 more minute.

When fragrant, add the sliced portobellos and cook for 3-4 more minutes, stirring occasionally.

Add the rest of the ingredients to the pot and give the mixture a good stir to combine. Cook for just another 2 minutes.

Let cool before storing.

Storing:

Store in airtight containers in the fridge. Consume within 3 days. To freeze, divide among 4 Ziploc bags and place in the freezer. Consume within 3 months. Thaw in the fridge overnight and heat in the microwave for a few minutes.

Nutrition facts per serving:

Calories 80, Protein 4g, Total Carbs 4.6g, Net Carbs 2g, Total Fat 4g, Saturated Fat 1g, Fiber 4g, Sodium 210mg

Spinach Ricotta Pie

Preparation time: 10 minutes | Cooking time: 25 minutes | Servings: 8

Ingredients:

½ cup chopped Onions
6 cups chopped Spinach
2 cups Ricotta Cheese
3 Eggs
1 tbsp Olive Oil
¼ cup grated Parmesan Cheese
1 Garlic Clove, minced
1 cup shredded Mozzarella Cheese
Salt and Pepper, to taste
1 ½ cups Water

Instructions:

Turn the Instant Pot on, set it to "SAUTE", and add the olive oil to it. When hot and sizzling, add the onions. Saute them for approximately 3 minutes. When softened, add the garlic clove and cook for just a minute, until fragrant. Stir in the kale and cook it for a minute or so, until it becomes wilted. Transfer the mixture to a bowl.

Pour the water into the Instant Pot and lower the trivet. Beat the eggs in the same bowl with the kale, and then stir in the remaining ingredients. Grab a dish that fits inside the Instant Pot and spray it with some cooking spray.

Pour the ricotta and kale mixture into the dish. Place the dish on top of the trivet and close the lid. Turn it clockwise to seal and then hit "MANUAL". Set the cooking time to 20 minutes. Cook on HIGH pressure.

When the timer goes off, press the "KEEP WARM/CANCEL" button. Turn the pressure handle from "Sealing" to "Venting" for a quick pressure release. Open the lid and remove the dish from the Instant Pot. Let cool before storing.

Storing:

Store in the fridge in airtight containers. Best if consumed within 5 days. To freeze, divide among 4 Ziploc bags and place in the freezer. Consume within 3 months. Thaw in the fridge overnight and consume at room temperature.

Nutrition facts per serving:

Calories 250, Protein 8g, Total Carbs 5.1g, Net Carbs 3.4g, Total Fat 15g, Saturated Fat 6g, Fiber 2.1g, Sodium 425mg

Smoked Paprika Cauliflower Cakes

Preparation time: 10 minutes | Cooking time: 8 minutes | Servings: 4

Ingredients:

1 pound Cauliflower Rice (processed in a food processor)
1 tsp Smoked Paprika
½ tsp Baking Powder
½ cup Almond Flour (or Flaxseed Meal if you prefer)
1 tsp Pepper
¼ tsp Garlic Powder
¼ tsp Onion Powder
3 Eggs
½ tsp Salt
½ cup Parmesan Cheese
2 tbsp Butter

Instructions:

Place all of the ingredients, except the butter, in a large bowl and mix with your hands well to combine. Shape the mixture into 4 cakes.

Turn the Instant Pot on and set it to "SAUTE". Add half of the butter and cook until it is melted.

Then, add two of the cauliflower cakes inside the Instant Pot and cook them on all sides until they become crispy.

Melt the remaining tablespoon of butter and repeat the process with the other two cakes. Let cool before storing.

Storing:

Divide cakes between 4 airtight containers. Place in the fridge and consume within 3 days. To freeze, divide among 4 Ziploc bags and place in the freezer. Consume within 3 months. Thaw in the fridge overnight and heat in the microwave for a few minutes.

Nutrition facts per serving:

Calories 210, Protein 9g, Total Carbs 5.5g, Net Carbs 3.5g, Total Fat 15g, Saturated Fat 4g, Fiber 1g, Sodium 450mg

Three-Cheese Stuffed Peppers

Preparation time: 15 minutes | Cooking time: 25 minutes | Servings: 4

Ingredients:

½ cup Cottage Cheese
½ cup grated Parmesan Cheese
½ cup shredded Mozzarella Cheese
¼ cup chopped Spinach
2 Bell Peppers
4 Eggs
Salt and Pepper, to taste
1 ½ cups Water

Instructions:

Pour the water into the Instant Pot and lower the trivet. Grease a baking dish that can fit inside the Instant Pot with some cooking spray and set aside.

Cut the bell peppers in half lengthwise and remove the seeds. Place all of the remaining ingredients in a bowl and mix well to combine. If you want to, you can do this step in a food processor until the mixture becomes smooth.

Divide the cheesy mixture between the bell peppers. Arrange the stuffed peppers in the baking dish and then place the dish on top of the trivet. Close the lid and turn clockwise to seal. Select the "MANUAL" cooking mode. Set the cooking time to 25 minutes. Cook on HIGH pressure.

After the beep, press the "KEEP WARM/CANCEL" button. Move the pressure handle to "Venting" to do a quick pressure release and open the lid carefully. Let cool before storing.

Storing:

Divide between 4 airtight containers. Place in the fridge and consume within 5 days. To freeze, divide among 4 Ziploc bags and place in the freezer. Consume within 3 months. Thaw in the fridge overnight and heat in the microwave for a few minutes.

Nutrition facts per serving:

Calories 245, Protein 18g, Total Carbs 4g, Net Carbs 2.5g, Total Fat 16g, Saturated Fat 5.5g, Fiber 1g, Sodium 380mg

Kale and Cauliflower Stew

Preparation time: 5 minutes | Cooking time: 12 minutes | Servings: 4

Ingredients:

2 Celery Stalks, diced
3 cups Cauliflower Rice
2 tbsp Olive Oil
2 Garlic Cloves, minced
2 Carrots, sliced
2 cups Kale, chopped
1 Onion, diced
4 cups Vegie Broth
14 ounces canned diced Tomatoes
2 tsp Cumin
Salt and Pepper, to taste

Instructions:

Set the Instant Pot to "SAUTE" and add the olive oil to it. When hot and sizzling, add the celery, onions, and carrots, and saute for a few minutes, until softened. Then, stir in the garlic and cook for additional 30-60 seconds.

Add the rest of the ingredients to the pot and stir to combine well. Put the lid on and turn it clockwise. The chiming sound means it has been sealed properly.

Select the "MANUAL" cooking mode and set the cooking time to 8 minutes. Cook on HIGH. When the timer goes off, press the "KEEP WARM/CANCEL" button. Let the pressure valve drop on its own for a natural pressure release. Open the lid gently and ladle into serving bowls.

Let cool before storing.

Storing:

Store in the fridge in airtight containers. Best if consumed within 3 days. To freeze, divide among 4 Ziploc bags and place in the freezer. Consume within 3 months. Thaw in the fridge overnight and heat in the microwave for a few minutes.

Nutrition facts per serving:

Calories 320, Protein 12g, Total Carbs 5.5g, Net Carbs 2.5g, Total Fat 14g, Saturated Fat 3g, Fiber 1.5g, Sodium 270mg

Spiced Radishes

Preparation time: 10 minutes | Cooking time: 8 minutes | Servings: 4

Ingredients:

16 Radishes, halved

2 tsp minced Garlic

¼ cup Olive Oil

1 tsp chopped Rosemary

½ tsp Red Pepper Flakes

Salt and Pepper, to taste

Instructions:

Set your Instant Pot to "SAUTE" and place the radishes inside. Dump all of the remaining ingredients inside and stir well to combine. "Roast" the radishes until they get a beautiful brown color and are caramelized well.

If you want the radishes to be softer, transfer them to a baking dish and pour about 1 ½ cups of water into the pot. Place the dish on the trivet and cook the radishes for about 3 minutes on "MANUAL" or HIGH. But they are just as delicious if left crunchier. Let cool before storing.

Storing:

Divide the pasta between 4 airtight containers. Place in the fridge and consume within 3 days. To freeze, divide among 4 Ziploc bags and place in the freezer. Consume within 3 months. Thaw in the fridge overnight and heat in the microwave for a few minutes.

Nutrition facts per serving:

Calories 100, Protein 1g, Total Carbs 2g, Net Carbs 1g, Total Fat 14g, Saturated Fat 2g, Fiber 1g, Sodium 210mg

Asparagus Zoodles with Pesto

Preparation time: 10 minutes | Cooking time: 5 minutes | Servings: 2

Ingredients:

4 Asparagus Spears, sliced

2 Zucchinis, spiralized

1 Garlic Clove, minced

2 tsp Olive Oil

¼ cup Pesto Sauce

Salt and Pepper, to taste

Instructions:

This is a SAUTÉ-only cooking method, so you don't need any liquid. Turn the Instant Pot on, set it to "SAUTE", and add the olive oil to it. When hot and sizzling, add the mince garlic.

Cook the garlic for just a minute, until it becomes fragrant. Stir in the asparagus and zoodles and cook for about 3 minutes. Season with some salt and pepper. Stir in the pesto sauce and cook just until it becomes heated through. Let cool before storing.

Storing:

Store in the fridge in airtight containers. Best if consumed within 3 days. To freeze, divide among 4 Ziploc bags and place in the freezer. Consume within 3 months. Thaw in the fridge overnight and heat in the microwave for a few minutes.

Nutrition facts per serving:

Calories 310, Protein 8g, Total Carbs 5g, Net Carbs 2g, Total Fat 25g, Saturated Fat 8g, Fiber 4g, Sodium 300mg

Radish Hash Browns

Preparation time: 5 minutes | Cooking time: 10 minutes | Servings: 4

Ingredients:

1 pound Radishes, shredded
⅓ cup grated Parmesan Cheese
¼ tsp Garlic Powder

Salt and Pepper, to taste
1 ½ cups Water

Instructions:

Pour the water into the Instant Pot and lower the trivet. Grease a baking dish with some cooking spray and set aside.In a large bowl, beat the eggs along with the garlic powder and some salt and pepper. Stir in the radishes and the parmesan cheese.

Pour the mixture into the greased baking dish and place the dish on top of the trivet. Close the lid of the Instant Pot and turn it clockwise. The chiming sound should indicate proper sealing. Select "MANUAL" and set the cooking time to 20 minutes. Cook on HIGH pressure.

When the timer goes off, press the "KEEP WARM/CANCEL" button. Turn the pressure handle to "Venting" and release the pressure quickly. Open the lid carefully. Cut the hash browns into 4 squares. Let cool before storing.

Storing:

Store in the fridge in 4 airtight containers. Best if consumed within 3 days. To freeze, divide among 4 Ziploc bags and place in the freezer. Consume within 3 months. Thaw in the fridge overnight and heat in the microwave for a few minutes.

Nutrition facts per serving:

Calories 80, Protein 7g, Total Carbs 5g, Net Carbs 3g, Total Fat 5g, Saturated Fat 1.5g, Fiber 2g, Sodium 180mg

Pressureless Porcini Risotto

Preparation time: 5 minutes | Cooking time: 17 minutes | Servings: 4

Ingredients:

1 Shallot, diced
4 ½ cups Cauliflower Rice
¼ cup Butter
3 ½ ounces grated Parmesan Cheese
1 tbsp chopped Basil
½ pound Porcini Mushrooms, sliced
3 tbsp Olive Oil
¼ cup Vegetable Broth
Salt and Pepper, to taste

Instructions:

Set the Instant Pot to "SAUTE" and add the olive oil to it. When hot and sizzling, add the porcini slices. Cook for about 4 minutes.

Transfer the mushrooms to a plate and add the shallots to the pot. Cook for 3 minutes.

Transfer the shallots to the bowl, as well. Add the cauliflower to the pot and pour the broth over. Cook on "SAUTE" for about 5 minutes, until soft.

Stir in the veggies and the rest of the ingredients. Let cool before storing.

Storing:

Store in the fridge in airtight containers. Best if consumed within 3 days. To freeze, divide among 4 Ziploc bags and place in the freezer. Consume within 3 months. Thaw in the fridge overnight and heat in the microwave for a few minutes.

Nutrition facts per serving:

Calories 265, Protein 11g, Total Carbs 5g, Net Carbs 2.5g, Total Fat 18g, Saturated Fat 8.5g, Fiber 2g, Sodium 370mg

DESSERT RECIPES

Cocoa Walnut Cake

Preparation time: 10 minutes | Cooking time: 20 minutes | Servings: 6

Ingredients:

1 cup Almond or Coconut Flour
3 Eggs
¼ cup chopped Walnuts
¼ cup Coconut Oil
¼ cup Cocoa Powder, unsweetened
⅔ cup Sweetener
⅓ cup Heavy Whipping Cream
1 tsp Baking Powder

Instructions:

Pour the water into your Instant Pot and lower the trivet.

Place all of the remaining ingredients in a large bowl and mix with an electric mixer until the mixture is well combined and fluffy.

Grease a cake pan with some cooking spray and pour the batter into it. Cover the pan with a piece of aluminum foil.

Place the pan on top of the trivet. Put the lid on and turn it clockwise to seal.

Select "MANUAL" and set the cooking time to 20 minutes. Cook on HIGH pressure.

After the beep, select the "KEEP WARM/CANCEL" button.

Release the pressure naturally, by letting the valve to drop on its own. Let cool completely.

Storing:

Store the cake at room temperature in airtight container for 3-4 days. To freeze, divide among 6 Ziploc bags and place in the freezer. Consume within 3 months. Thaw in the fridge overnight and let reach room temperature.

Nutrition facts per serving:

Calories 300, Protein 11g, Total Carbs 10g, Net Carbs 3g, Total Fat 28g, Saturated Fat 14g, Fiber 3g, Sodium 140mg

Lemony Ricotta Cake

Preparation time: 10 minutes | Cooking time: 30 minutes | Servings: 6

Ingredients:

Ingredients:
8 ounces Cream Cheese
⅓ cup Ricotta Cheese
¼ cup Sweetener
1 tsp Lemon Zest
Juice of 1 Lemon
2 Eggs
1 ½ cups Water

Topping:

1 tsp Sweetener
2 tbsp Sour Cream

Instructions:

Pour the water into your Instant Pot and lower the trivet. Place the first 5 ingredients in a bowl, and mix with an electric mixer until the mixture is well-combined and with no lumps. Then, add the eggs inside and mix them into the ricotta mixture briefly, just until the mixture is fully combined. Otherwise, your crust will be cracked at the end.

Pour the batter into a greased springform pan that fits in the Instant Pot, and cover with a piece of aluminum foil. Place the pan on top of the trivet and close the lid. Turn it clockwise to seal. Select "MANUAL" and set the cooking time to 30 minutes. Cook on HIGH pressure.

After the beep, select the "KEEP WARM/CANCEL" button. Do a natural pressure release by letting the valve drop on its own.

Finally, whisk together the sour cream and sweetener and spread over the cake. Let cool completely. Slice into 6 pieces.

Storing:

Store the cake at room temperature in airtight container for 3-4 days. To freeze, divide among 6 Ziploc bags and place in the freezer. Consume within 3 months. Thaw in the fridge overnight and let reach room temperature.

Nutrition facts per serving:

Calories 180, Protein 5g, Total Carbs 3g, Net Carbs 2 g, Total Fat 16g, Saturated Fat 10g, Fiber 1g, Sodium 100mg

Chocolate Mini Cakes

Preparation time: 10 minutes | Cooking time: 9 minutes | Servings: 2

Ingredients:

1 tsp Vanilla Extract
2 tbsp Splenda
2 tbsp Heavy Cream
¼ cup Cocoa Powder, unsweetened
2 Eggs
1 ½ cups Water

Instructions:

Pour the water into the Instant Pot and lower the trivet.

Grease 2 ramekins with some cooking spray and set aside.

Whisk the dry ingredients in one bowl, and the wet ones in another one.

Gently combine the two mixtures, making sure the batter is smooth and well-combined.

Pour the batter into the ramekins. Place the ramekins on top of the trivet and close the lid. Turn the lid clockwise to seal.

Select "MANUAL" and set the cooking time to 9 minutes. Make sure to cook on HIGH pressure.

After the beep, select the "KEEP WARM/CANCEL" button.

Turn the pressure handle to "Venting" for a quick pressure release and open the lid carefully. Flip the cakes onto plates. Let cool before slicing.

Storing:

Store in the fridge in an airtight container. Consume within 3 days. To freeze, divide among 2 Ziploc bags and place in the freezer. Consume within the next 3 months. Thaw in the fridge overnight.

Nutrition facts per serving:

Calories 230, Protein 6g, Total Carbs 4g, Net Carbs 3.5g, Total Fat 7g, Saturated Fat 2.2g, Fiber 0.5g, Sodium 150mg

Rum Mug Cake

Preparation time: 10 minutes | Cooking time: 10 minutes | Servings: 1

Ingredients:

1 Egg
⅓ cup Almond Flour
Pinch of Salt

½ tsp Rum Extract
1 tbsp Sweetener
1 ½ cups Water

Instructions:

Pour the water into the Instant Pot and lower the trivet. Place all of the ingredients in ab owl and whisk well to combine the mixture well. Grab a mason jar and pour the batter into it. Seal the jar and place it on top of the trivet. Put the lid on and turn it clockwise to seal. Select "MANUAL" and set the cooking time to 10 minutes. Cook on HIGH pressure.

After the beep, select the "KEEP WARM/CANCEL" button. Release the pressure quickly by moving the handle to "Venting". Open the lid carefully. Allow the mug cake to cool before slicing.

Storing:

Store at room temperature in airtight containers. To freeze, divide among Ziploc bag and place in the freezer. Consume within 3 months. Thaw in the fridge overnight and bring to room temperature before consuming.

Nutrition facts per serving:

Calories 210, Protein 5g, Total Carbs 3g, Net Carbs 2g, Total Fat 6.5g, Saturated Fat 1.5g, Fiber 1g, Sodium 180mg

Lemon Curd

Preparation time: 10 minutes | Cooking time: 20 minutes | Servings: 3

Ingredients:

3 ounces Butter, at room temperature
⅔ cup Lime Juice
1 cup Sweetener
2 Eggs plus 2 Egg Yolks

1 ½ tsp Lime Zest

1 ½ cups Water

Instructions:

Place the sweetener and butter in your food processor and process for 2 minutes. Then, add the eggs and egg yolks and mix for 1 more minute. Stir in the zest and juice until the mixture is well combined. Divide the mixture between 3 half-pint mason jars.Pour the water into your Instant Pot and lower the trivet. Arrange the jars on top of the trivet and close the lid.

Turn it clockwise for a proper sealing. Select "MANUAL" after the chime, and set the cooking time to 10 minutes. Cook on HIGH pressure. After the beep, select the "KEEP WARM/ CANCEL" button. Let the valve drop on its own for a natural pressure release. Allow to cool completely.

Storing:

Store in an airtight container at room temperature. The curd can be enjoyed for up to a week if kept in the fridge. To freeze, divide among 3 Ziploc bags and place in the freezer. Consume within the next 3 months. Thaw in the fridge overnight and let heat to room temperature to consume.

Nutrition facts per serving:

Calories 280, Protein 7g, Total Carbs 5.6g, Total Fat 8.4g, Saturated Fat 4g, Fiber 4g, Sodium 420mg

Vanilla Bean Cheesecake

Preparation time: 10 minutes | Cooking time: 10 minutes | Servings: 8

Ingredients:

½ cup Swerve
2 Eggs
1 Vanilla Bean, scraped

16 ounces Cream Cheese
1 tsp Vanilla Extract
1 ½ cups Water

Instructions:

Pour the water into the Instant Pot and lower the trivet. Place all of the ingredients in a food processor (or a blender) and process until the mixture becomes smooth. Grab a cake pan (preferably a 7-inch one), grease it with some cooking spray and pour the batter into it. Cover the pan with a piece of aluminum foil and then place it on top of the trivet. Put the lid on and turn it clockwise to seal properly. After the chime, select "MANUAL" and set the cooking time to 20 minutes. Cook on HIGH pressure.

After the beep, select the "KEEP WARM/CANCEL" button. Release the pressure naturally, by allowing the valve to drop on its own and let cool before slicing.

Storing:

Store in an airtight container at room temperature. Consume for 3 days. To freeze, divide among four Ziploc bags and place in the freezer. Consume within 3 months. Thaw in the fridge overnight and bring to room temperature before consuming.

Nutrition facts per serving:

Calories 245, Protein 9g, Total Carbs 4g, Net Carbs 3g, Total Fat 8g, Saturated Fat 2g, Fiber 1g, Sodium 140mg

Lavender and Apple Cake

Preparation time: 10 minutes | Cooking time: 25 minutes | Servings: 6

Ingredients:

⅓ cup Butter, melted
2 tbsp Coconut Flour
2 tbsp Lemon Juice
4 small Gala Apples, peeled and cut into slices
½ tsp dried Lavender flowers
1 tsp Vanilla Extract
⅔ cup Cassav Flour
¼ cup Almond Flour
½ tsp Baking Powder
1 tbsp Gelatin Powder
Pinch of Salt
2 cups Water

Instructions:

Pour the water into the Instant Pot and lower the trivet. Line a cake pan with a piece or parchment paper and set aside. Combine the apples, lemon juice, and lavender, in a bowl, and then arrange the apple slices at the bottom of the lined pan.

Combine the dry ingredients in one bowl and whisk together the rest of the ingredients in another bowl. Combine the two mixtures gently and then pour the batter over the apple slices. Grab a piece of aluminum foil and cover the pan with it.

Place the pan on top of the trivet and close the lid of the Instant Pot. Seal the Instant Pot by turning the lid clockwise until you hear the chime.

Select "MANUAL" and set the cooking time to 25 minutes. Cook on HIGH pressure. After the beep, select the "KEEP WARM/CANCEL" button. Allow the valve to drop on its own for a natural pressure release. Allow to cool before slicing.

Storing:

Store in airtight containers at room temperature. To freeze, divide among Ziploc bags and place in the freezer. Consume within 3 months. Thaw in the fridge overnight and bring to room temperature to consume.

Nutrition facts per serving:

Calories 285, Protein 5g, Total Carbs 7g, Net Carbs 5.5g, Total Fat 4g, Saturated Fat 1g, Fiber 1.5g, Sodium 125mg

Chocolate and Applesauce Pudding Cake

Preparation time: 10 minutes | Cooking time: 10 minutes | Servings: 4

Ingredients:

½ cup Sugar-Free Applesauce
1 tsp Vanilla Extract
⅔ cup chopped Dark Chocolate, melted
3 tbsp Cocoa Powder, unsweetened
2 Eggs
¼ cup Arrowroot
Pinch of Salt
1 ½ cups Water

Instructions:

Pour the water into your Instant Pot and lower the trivet. Grease a baking pan (preferably a 6-inch one) with some cooking spray and set it aside.

Place all of the ingredients in a large bowl and whisk well until the mixture is smooth and with no lumps. Pour the batter into the prepared baking pan.

Grab a piece of aluminum foil and cover the pan with it. Place the pan on top of the trivet and close the lid of the Instant Pot.

To seal the Instant Pot, just turn the lid clockwise until you hear the chime.

Press the "MANUAL" button and set the cooking time to 10 minutes. Cook on HIGH pressure.

When the timer goes off, select the "KEEP WARM/CANCEL" button. Move the pressure handle from "Sealing" to "Venting" for a quick pressure release and open the lid carefully. Let cool completely.

Storing:

Divide between glass jars, seal, and store in the fridge. Consume within 3 days. To freeze, divide among freezer cups with lids. Thaw in the fridge overnight and consume cold.

Nutrition facts per serving:

Calories 155, Protein 4g, Total Carbs 5.1g, Net Carbs 3.2g, Total Fat 9g, Saturated Fat 4.5g, Fiber 2.8g, Sodium 110mg

Very Chocolate Cheesecake

Preparation time: 15 minutes | Cooking time: 25 minutes | Servings: 8

Ingredients:

¼ cup Coconut Flour
¼ cup Almond Flour
1 ½ tbsp Sweetener
2 ½ tbsp Cocoa Powder, unsweetened
2 tbsp Butter, melted
1 ½ cups Water

Filling:

16 ounces Cream Cheese, softened
1 Egg plus 2 Egg Yolks
⅓ cup Cocoa Powder, unsweetened
½ tsp Stevia Powder
¾ cup Heavy Cream
1 tsp Vanilla Extract
¼ cup Sour Cream
½ tsp Monk Fruit Powder
6 ounces Dark Chocolate, melted

Instructions:

Pour the water into the Instant Pot and line a cake pan with a piece of parchment paper. Lower the trivet.

Combine all of the crust ingredients together in a bow, and press the mixture into the lined pan.

Place all of the filling ingredients in a blender or a food processor and pulse until the mixture is blended and smooth. Pour the filling over the crust. Grab a piece of aluminum foil and cover the pan well.

Make a sling with the foil and place the pan over the sling so you can easily remove it from the Instant Pot afterwards. Place the pan on top of the trivet and close the lid. Seal by turning clockwise. Select "MANUAL" and set the cooking time to 20 minutes. Cook on HIGH pressure.

After the beep, select the "KEEP WARM/CANCEL" button. Release the pressure naturally by allowing the valve to drop on its own.

Storing:

Store at room temperature in airtight containers. To freeze, divide among Ziploc bags and place in the freezer. Consume within 3 months. Thaw in the fridge overnight and bring to room temperature to consume.

Nutrition facts per serving:

Calories 402, Protein 8g, Total Carbs 21g, Net Carbs 8g, Total Fat 38 g, Saturated Fat 22g, Fiber 13g, Sodium 60mg

Strawberry Cobbler Mock

Preparation time: 10 minutes | Cooking time: 10 minutes | Servings: 4

Ingredients:

1 cup chopped Strawberries
2 tsp Lemon Juice
5 Egg Yolks
¼ tsp Baking Powder
½ tsp Lemon Zest

4 tbsp Sweetener
¼ cup Almond Flour
2 tbsp Heavy Cream
2 tbsp Butter
2 cups Water

Instructions:

Pour the water into the Instant Pot and lower the trivet. Grease a cake pan that first inside the Instant Pot, with some cooking spray; Set aside.

Place all of the dry ingredients in a bowl and whisk together until they are combined. In another bowl, whisk together the wet ingredients until smooth. Combine the two mixtures gently, until they are no more lumps visible. Stir in the strawberries and pour the batter into the prepared cake pan. Put the lid on and turn it clockwise to seal. Select "MANUAL" and set the cooking time to 15 minutes. Cook on HIGH pressure.

After the beep, select the "KEEP WARM/CANCEL" button. Turn the pressure handle to "Venting" for a quick pressure release, open the lid carefully and allow to cool completely.

Storing:

Store in the fridge in airtight containers and consume within 3 days. To freeze, divide between Ziploc bags, or freezer molds, and freeze for up to 3 months. Thaw overnight in the fridge and consume cold.

Nutrition facts per serving:

Calories 440, Protein 9g, Total Carbs 6g, Net Carbs 2.5g, Total Fat 42g, Saturated Fat 25g, Fiber 4g, Sodium 75mg

CONCLUSION

Following a strict diet such as the Ketogenic one can be truly challenging. And while it is true that this eating plan can transform our physical and mental health tremendously, when life's obligations have us in a constant rush, sticking to the no-carb rule can be pretty overwhelming. But not if you know the easiest way to maintaining the Keto lifestyle.

Combining the most revolutionary kitchen appliance - the instant pot, with one of the most popular and super successful diets today - the ketogenic diet, this book will reveal to you the secrets of easy Keto cooking, weight losing, and taste-bud-pleasing.

Quick, healthy, and without having to spend hours in front of the stove, Instant Keto cooking is the best guarantee that you will reap out the Ketogenic benefits without sacrificing meal satisfaction.

Providing you with carefully selected delightful recipes, this cookbook is a definite must-have for those who own an Instant Pot, want to enter or maintain Ketosis, and ideally, both.

Now, jump to the first recipe and see how delicious low-carb meals can be when cooked under pressure.

Made in the USA
Lexington, KY
10 August 2018